CIVIL WAR WEAPONS

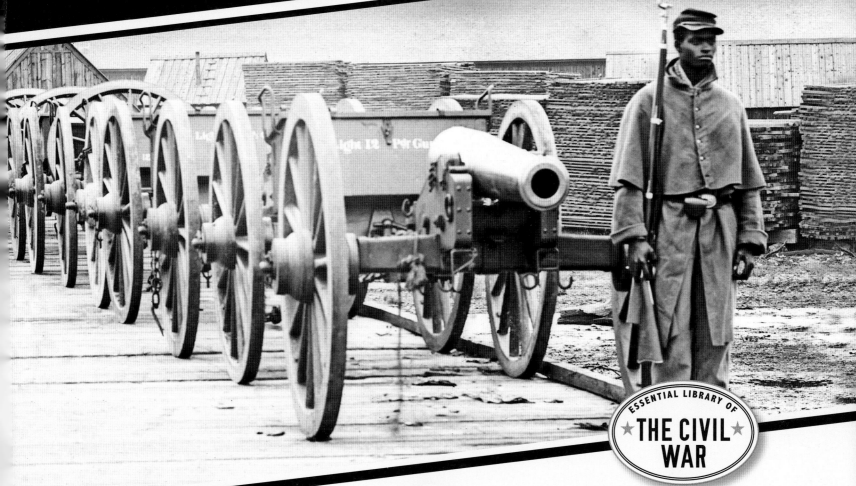

ESSENTIAL LIBRARY OF
★ THE CIVIL ★
WAR

Essential Library

An Imprint of Abdo Publishing
abdopublishing.com

BY NEL YOMTOV

CONTENT CONSULTANT
LANCE JANDA, CHAIR
DEPARTMENT OF HISTORY AND GOVERNMENT
CAMERON UNIVERSITY

abdopublishing.com

Published by Abdo Publishing, a division of ABDO, PO Box 398166, Minneapolis, Minnesota 55439. Copyright © 2017 by Abdo Consulting Group, Inc. International copyrights reserved in all countries. No part of this book may be reproduced in any form without written permission from the publisher. Essential Library™ is a trademark and logo of Abdo Publishing.

Printed in the United States of America, North Mankato, Minnesota
052016
092016

THIS BOOK CONTAINS
RECYCLED MATERIALS

Cover Photo: Buyenlarge/Getty Images
Interior Photos: Buyenlarge/Getty Images, 1, 72, 80; Don Troiani/Corbis, 4, 14, 39, 40; Mathew B. Brady/AP Images, 7, 98 (bottom); Library of Congress, 11, 18, 32, 43, 52, 54, 58, 82, 87, 94; Scientific American, 21; Alfred R. Waud/Library of Congress, 23, 74; Edwin Wildman, 26; Corbis, 28, 76; Medford Historical Society Collection/Corbis, 36; David Knox/Library of Congress, 45; James F. Gibson/Library of Congress, 47; West Point Museum Collection, United States Military Academy, 50, 98 (top); Lebrecht Music & Arts/Lebrecht Music & Arts/Corbis, 61; Bruce Smith/AP Images, 65, 99 (bottom); MPI/Getty Images, 66; Timothy H. O'Sullivan/Library of Congress, 69; A. J. Russell/Getty Images, 84; Mathew B. Brady/Library of Congress, 92, 99 (top); Alexander Gardner/Library of Congress, 97

Editor: Arnold Ringstad
Series Designers: Kelsey Oseid and Maggie Villaume

Cataloging-in-Publication Data

Names: Yomtov, Nel, author.
Title: Civil War weapons / by Nel Yomtov.
Description: Minneapolis, MN : Abdo Publishing, [2017] | Series: Essential library
    of the Civil War | Includes bibliographical references and index.
Identifiers: LCCN 2015960310 | ISBN 9781680782783 (lib. bdg.) |
    ISBN 9781680774672 (ebook)
Subjects: LCSH: United States--History--Civil War, 1861-1865--Equipment and
    supplies--Juvenile literature. | United States. Army--Weapons system--
    History--19th century--Juvenile literature. | Confederate States of America.
    Army--Weapons systems--Juvenile literature. | United States--History--Civil
    War, 1861-1865--Technology--Juvenile literature. | Military weapons--United
    States--History--19th century--Juvenile literature.
Classification: DDC 973.7/8--dc23
LC record available at http://lccn.loc.gov/2015960310

CONTENTS

CHAPTER 1   TOOLS OF DESTRUCTION...4

CHAPTER 2   THE CAVALRY AND ITS WEAPONS 14

CHAPTER 3   THE INFANTRY AND ITS WEAPONS...........................28

CHAPTER 4   ARTILLERY 40

CHAPTER 5   THE NAVAL WAR 54

CHAPTER 6   FORTS AND FORTIFICATIONS................................. 66

CHAPTER 7   BATTLE TACTICS 76

CHAPTER 8   THE FIRST MODERN WAR 84

TIMELINE 98
ESSENTIAL FACTS..100
GLOSSARY 102
ADDITIONAL RESOURCES....................................104
SOURCE NOTES...106
INDEX..110
ABOUT THE AUTHOR..112

The battles of the Civil War, including Antietam, were fought with weapons that made the war the bloodiest conflict in the nation's history.

CHAPTER
★ 1 ★

TOOLS OF DESTRUCTION

As dawn broke on the morning of September 17, 1862, the deafening roar of gunfire abruptly awakened US Army private David Thompson of the Ninth New York Infantry. Thompson and his weary Union comrades were positioned near a stone bridge that crossed Antietam Creek in Maryland. Confederate artillery batteries and a regiment of Confederate infantrymen were stationed across the creek.

As the morning wore on, the firing grew louder and more intense. Suddenly, silence fell over the battlefield. The young infantryman sensed the time to enter the action had come. A Union officer rose from his crouched position and threw his right arm into the air. He waved his arm and ordered his troops forward.

Leaving their knapsacks, Thompson and his fellow soldiers pressed across a field toward the Confederate position. As they advanced, enemy bullets whizzed inches above their heads. To avoid the deadly hail, Thompson's unit threw themselves on the ground.

At that moment, Confederate artillery opened fire on the Union soldiers. The thundering of smoothbore cannons firing 12-pound (5.4 kg) projectiles echoed across the entire battlefield. Thompson, lying facedown in the muddy field, looked up. He saw a dreadful sight. Grapeshot—a mass of metal balls wrapped in a canvas sack that spread through the air when shot from a cannon—had struck a fellow Union soldier in the skull. The man was instantly killed. But Thompson barely had time to gather his thoughts as the order to charge ahead arrived.

The Union regiment rose and advanced onward. In a second, the air was full of the hiss of Confederate bullets and the flash of deadly artillery gunfire. The entire landscape seemed to turn red with blood. In 12 hours of brutal combat, roughly 23,000 Americans were killed, wounded, or missing.[1] The deadly weapons used during the American Civil War (1861–1865), ranging from handheld muskets and rifles to enormous artillery pieces, made Antietam the bloodiest one-day battle in the history of the nation. David Thompson was among the lucky soldiers to survive it.

The aftermath of the Battle of Antietam made it clear how destructive modern warfare could be.

THE LEGACY OF THE CIVIL WAR

Few conflicts in history continue to capture as much interest as the American Civil War. One of the main reasons for this popularity is the incredible array of Civil War weapons that have survived for more than 150 years. Thousands of handguns, muskets and rifles, cannons, grenades, land and sea mines, and many other weapons are on display at museums and battlefield centers. Additionally, private individuals and government institutions hold countless weapons in their collections.

NORTHERN AND SOUTHERN ECONOMIES

By the eve of war in the spring of 1861, the North was well established as a manufacturing economy. Ninety percent of America's manufacturing production came from Northern states. As the North became more mechanized, production of major goods soared. Northern states produced most of the nation's textiles, raw iron, and leather. Northern factories produced 32 times more firearms than Southern manufacturers. The North possessed nearly 70 percent of the nation's railroad tracks, vital for carrying troops, supplies, and weapons. By contrast, the South's economy was mainly agricultural. Relying on slave labor, Southern states produced two-thirds of the world's cotton but had limited manufacturing capability.[2] With most of its wealth based on a slave economy rather than on factories, railroads, and mechanized farming, the South found it difficult to wage a long war.

Another important reason for ongoing interest in the war is photography. This technology was in its infancy when the Civil War began. Hundreds of thousands of photographs of weapons, uniforms, soldiers, officers, and equipment are available for study. For both serious students of the war and those with a casual interest, there is an abundance of images to examine and explore.

The Civil War was fought between the US government, called the Union, and a group of states that broke off to form the Confederate States of America, or the Confederacy. Geographically, the Union was made up of states in the northern part of the United States. The Confederacy was composed of 11 states in the southern part of the country.

By the time the war ended with the Confederate surrender in April 1865, the fighting had raged over mountains, plains, forests, rivers, and seas. Battles were fought in large cities, small towns, villages, and remote wilderness settings.

The devastation was widespread. During the war, soldiers suffered an estimated 1.1 million casualties. The Union suffered roughly 596,670 casualties, including an estimated 365,000 deaths. Confederate casualties numbered more than 490,000, approximately 260,000 of them deaths. Roughly 2 percent of the total US population, approximately 625,000 people, lost their lives.[3] In some estimates, the Civil War death toll rises as high as 750,000.[4]

THE TOOLS OF WAR

The men who fought in the Civil War—farmers, students, laborers, lawyers, doctors, craftsmen, and others from a wide variety of occupations—were issued handguns, rifles, swords, cannons, and other tools of warfare. Few had ever used such arms before. Each one had to be instructed how to use the weapons safely and effectively.

Many of the weapons used in the conflict were manufactured in the United States. Others came from the United Kingdom, France, and other European nations. Weapons designers from the North and the South constantly tried to

WHO FOUGHT IN THE CIVIL WAR?

Northern and Southern soldiers had very similar backgrounds. The soldiers of the Union army generally ranged in age from 18 to 45, with most under 30. Approximately half of the Union soldiers were farmers. Laborers, mechanics, teachers, doctors, and a wide range of other workers came from the industrial cities. Most of the Union soldiers had at least some schooling. Approximately one-quarter of the Union army was made up of men not born in the United States. Until May 1863, all Union soldiers were white. At that time, the US War Department established the Bureau of Colored Troops, which allowed African-American men to serve in the military.

Most Confederate soldiers were also under 30. More than half were farmers, but few owned slaves.[5] As in the Union army, soldiers came from a variety of jobs, including clerks, craftsmen, laborers, and students. Illiteracy was more common among Confederate soldiers than their Union counterparts. Foreign-born soldiers also fought for the South, though in much smaller numbers than those who fought for the Union. African-American men were not allowed to serve as soldiers until March 1865. However, they contributed to the Confederate war effort by building roads and bridges, digging ditches, and growing crops.

gain the upper hand by producing high-quality guns and other weapons. The industrial strength of the North, however, gave the Union an edge. Throughout the war, Southern designers and machinists struggled to keep pace with their Northern foes. For this reason, the South depended more heavily on captured weapons and those imported from Europe than the North.

When the war started, both sides scrambled to equip the thousands of untrained, inexperienced men who had volunteered to fight. Fewer than

Vast numbers of men needed to be armed and trained in the early months of the war.

40,000 modern rifles, designed with spiral-grooved barrels to make bullets spin for greater accuracy and distance, were available in the United States.[6] Most of these were stored in state arsenals or in US government armories, such as Harpers Ferry in Virginia. In time, the Confederate army seized many of these strongholds in Southern states. When weapon supplies were limited, the

North and the South were often forced to provide their troops with older arms, including muskets dating to the American Revolutionary War (1775–1783) era.

HARPERS FERRY

The Harpers Ferry Armory and Arsenal was located in Virginia on land bounded by the Potomac and Shenandoah Rivers. Established in 1799, the US government–owned facility manufactured weapons of all types, including muskets, rifles, and handguns. In October 1859, abolitionist John Brown led an armed band of antislavery crusaders in a raid on the arsenal. Brown's plan was to establish an armed resistance movement of freed slaves in the nearby mountains. He was captured by forces led by Robert E. Lee, who would later become the top Confederate general. Brown was then tried and hanged for treason, but he became a hero to many Northern abolitionists. The raid increased Southern fears of slave rebellions and inflamed growing tensions between the North and the South. Weeks after the outbreak of the Civil War in April 1861, Southern forces seized the armory's weapons and machinery before burning its buildings.

TECHNOLOGY IS KING

By 1861, the development and production of weapons had entered a new phase. Modern thinking and new manufacturing processes were about to revolutionize Civil War combat. On land, the accuracy and range of handguns, rifles, and artillery improved. On the sea, armored ships called ironclads foreshadowed the eventual end of wooden navies. In the air, spotters in surveillance balloons sometimes observed enemy strength and troop movements.

This advanced technology resulted in the creation of new military weapons capable of mass destruction and previously unimaginable mayhem. These weapons helped make the Civil War the bloodiest conflict in American history. In four years of combat, more Americans died than in all of the nation's other wars from the Revolutionary War through the Korean War (1950–1953) combined.[7]

MAKING MODERN AMERICA

The Civil War defined America as a nation. It preserved the Union and saved the democratic form of government and the rights and freedoms people enjoy today. It led to the end of slavery in the United States and set the country on a path toward fulfilling the statement in the Declaration of Independence that "all men are created equal."[8]

The United States had to go to war against itself to achieve these worthy accomplishments. The weapons of the North and South, combined with the courage and determination of the soldiers who carried them, made the brutal conflict possible.

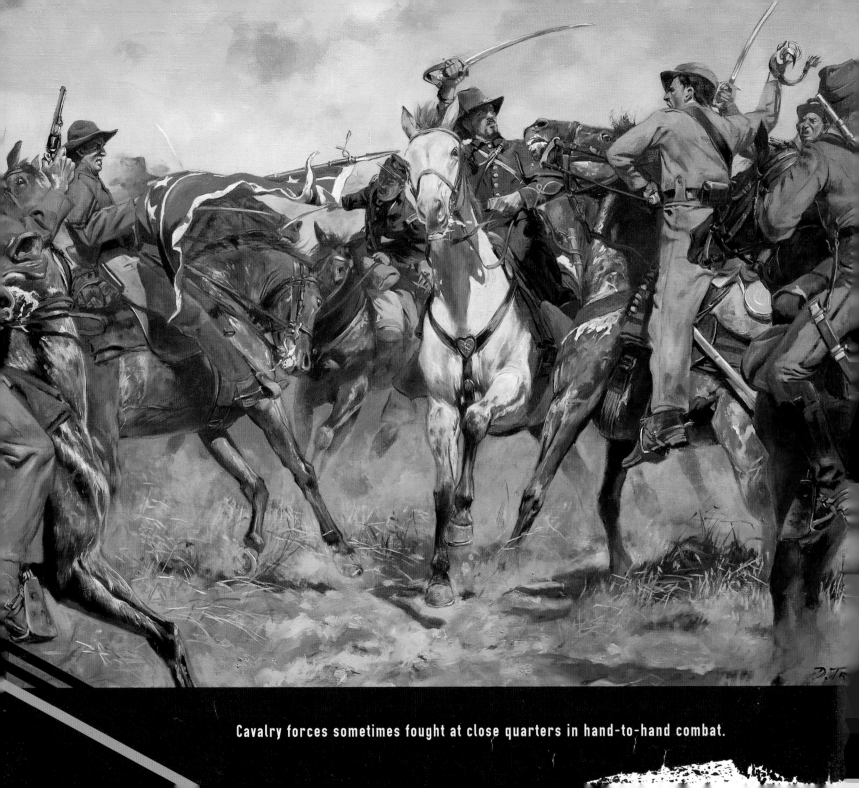

Cavalry forces sometimes fought at close quarters in hand-to-hand combat.

THE CAVALRY AND ITS WEAPONS

In modern armies, the word *cavalry* refers to troops who fight in armored vehicles. But in the past, the cavalry was the part of an army that fought on horseback. During the Civil War, large bodies of cavalry units saw action. At first, some military leaders in both the North and South were reluctant to accept cavalry regiments. In the early months of combat, cavalry units patrolled, scouted, and guarded supply trains and railroad depots. If they saw action at all, it was generally as shock troops, employing hit-and-run tactics to confuse and scatter the enemy. As the months passed, however, the use of cavalry on the battlefield became inevitable.

At the war's outset, the South held an edge in both the quality and leadership of its cavalry. Southern soldiers generally had more experience with horses and riding than their Northern counterparts. For soldiers who grew up in the mainly agricultural South, horses were a necessary part of life. By 1863, however, Northerners had established an effective cavalry that eventually surpassed the Confederates. By this time, the Southern cavalry was declining due to battlefield losses, disease, and a lack of quality horses.

JOHN MOSBY, CONFEDERATE CAVALRYMAN

John Singleton Mosby was a Confederate cavalry commander who organized and led a group of riders called Mosby's Raiders. The Raiders became famous for their lightning-quick attacks on unsuspecting Union troops. The Raiders' objectives were to disrupt Northern supply lines, capture Union messengers, and provide intelligence about the enemy's strength and positions in Virginia. Mosby's unit would strike Union forces swiftly and then rapidly scatter to avoid capture. The ability to attack quickly and vanish earned Mosby the nickname "Gray Ghost."

A charge by two opposing cavalry forces shattered the senses of everyone on the battlefield. The thunder of rushing hooves and the clatter of weapons and equipment combined with the roar of men's voices to produce an ear-splitting wall of sound. Clouds of thick dust kicked up as the two opposing armies drew nearer to each other. Then came the sounds of riders clashing and slashing at each other with their glistening sabers. The cavalry charge was the ultimate display of power, courage, and relentless movement.

Civil War military leaders initially used cavalry to gather information about the opponents' strength, position, and movement. As the number of cavalry increased, they became more active and aggressive. Units conducted surprise attacks, disrupted enemy communications and supply lines, and even destroyed trains carrying enemy supplies, weapons, and soldiers. The cavalry of both sides were typically equipped with three weapons: the sword, the carbine, and the pistol.

SWORDS

Both the North and the South put great effort and expense into the manufacture of edged weapons such as swords and bayonets. On the battlefield, cavalry troopers often charged into battle on horseback and then dismounted to fight on foot with their weapons. The saber was the traditional cavalry sword. It had a thick back edge to provide strength when used by a rider in a long, sweeping blow.

Union sabers were divided into two types: light and heavy. The light cavalry saber Model 1860 had a 35-inch (89 cm) blade with a large curve.[1] The blade measured 1 inch (2.5 cm) across. The heavy cavalry saber Model 1840 had a slightly straighter blade. It measured 37.5 inches (95 cm) long and 1.5 inches (3.3 cm) wide.[2] Both models had brass hilts, or handles, and wooden grips wrapped in leather bands with thin strips of copper wire. The swords were

carried in protective metal scabbards. During the war, the Union bought roughly 203,000 light and 189,100 heavy sabers.[3]

The Confederates used swords based largely on Union designs. The quality was typically poorer due to manufacturing limitations in the South. The blades were not finished as finely, and the grips were slightly less secure. It was not uncommon for Confederate cavalrymen to replace their own equipment with Union sabers and scabbards taken from the battlefield. In addition, some Confederate troopers were issued foreign swords, such as the British Pattern 1853 cavalry saber or those produced by German sword makers.

Early in the war, some Union and Confederate cavalry also carried lances, a throwback to medieval warfare. Lances

A Union soldier poses with a Model 1860 light cavalry saber.

SMOOTHBORE AND RIFLED WEAPONS

A smoothbore weapon has a barrel that is completely smooth on the inside. When the weapon fires, the projectile moves rapidly down the length of the barrel. As the projectile moves, it spins in an unpredictable way that often makes it slightly curve or tumble in flight. This effect makes smoothbore weapons somewhat inaccurate. Many types of weapons used during the Civil War were smoothbores.

Rifled weapons have spiral grooves cut into the inside of the barrel. As the projectile moves down the barrel, the grooves grip the sides of the projectile and spin it as it exits. This increases accuracy and range significantly. Rifled handguns, artillery, and shoulder-carried weapons were common during the war. They were more expensive and often took longer to reload, but they were much more effective on the battlefield.

generally were made from ash or Norwegian fir. They were fitted with sharp iron or steel spear tips. By 1863, the use of lances in combat was abandoned. New technologies were making guns and artillery deadlier than ever. Massed cavalry charges in the face of blistering enemy fire were no longer used. Dismounting, fighting on foot, then remounting to fight again became the preferred cavalry battle tactic. As a result, the carbine and pistol were the troopers' weapons of choice.

CARBINES

A carbine is a shorter and lighter version of a standard rifle. Civil War carbines were approximately 38 inches (96 cm) long, much smaller than the 56-inch (142 cm) rifled musket the infantry used.[4] Easier to handle and with a higher rate of fire, carbines were ideal for cavalry actions. Approximately 30 different types of carbines were used during the war.[5]

The standard Union cavalry carbine was the US Pistol Carbine Model 1855, a single-shot, breech-loaded weapon. A breech-loaded weapon is one that is loaded at the rear end of the gun barrel. It was carried in a saddle holster and fired with one hand while on horseback. To use the weapon while dismounted, the trooper removed a separate shoulder brace from another holster and attached it to the butt of the gun. The weapon then functioned as a carbine. Approximately 8,000 of this model of carbine were manufactured.[6]

Many Union cavalry units preferred the Spencer repeating rifle. Rather than firing a single bullet and then needing to be reloaded after each shot, the Spencer could fire several bullets in succession. A tube with seven cartridges, or rounds of ammunition, was placed into a small opening in the butt of the gun. A spring in

SPENCER'S REPEATING RIFLE

The inventor of the Spencer repeating rifle was 20-year-old Christopher M. Spencer. Born in Manchester, Connecticut, Spencer learned the firearms trade working at Samuel Colt's Patent Manufacturing Company in nearby Hartford. In 1860, Spencer received the patent for his breech-loading repeating rifle. In mid-1861, Spencer sold 700 rifles to the Union navy.[7] Spencer wanted to increase his sales to the government, however, and on August 18, 1863, he gave a demonstration of his rifle to the commander in chief, President Abraham Lincoln. Near the site of the partially completed Washington Monument, Lincoln personally test-fired the weapon and was pleased with its performance. The president ordered US military authorities to acquire the weapon immediately. By the end of the war, the government had purchased approximately 94,000 Spencers.[8]

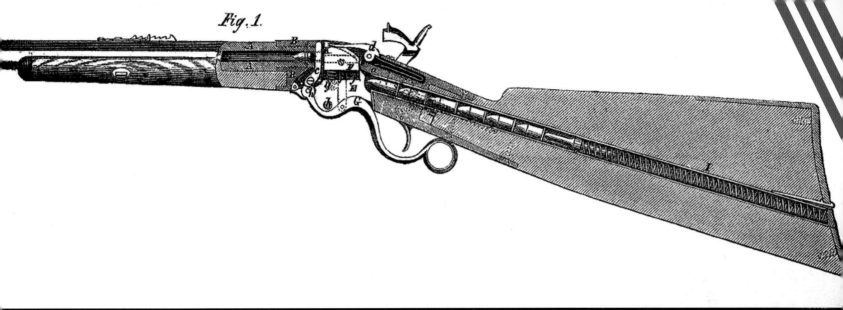

Fig. 1.

A contemporary diagram shows the inner workings of the Spencer carbine, including the spring-loaded tube that pushed cartridges into position for firing.

the tube pushed the cartridges forward. When the trigger of the gun was pulled, the cartridge was fired. Operating a lever ejected the empty ammunition casing and loaded the next round. The first known use of the Spencer carbine was in June 1863 by Colonel John Thomas Wilder's Lightning Brigade. Armed with these weapons, Wilder's men captured a key mountain pass from Confederate forces in central Tennessee.

The most popular carbine of the war was the Sharps M1859 single-shot breechloader. The Sharps was an accurate weapon. Like most carbines, its effective range was approximately 400 to 500 yards (366 to 457 m), the length of four to five football fields. The Sharps Rifle Company manufactured more than 30,000 M1859 carbines during the war.[9] The Union bought more than 80,000 Sharps carbines of all types at a value of roughly $2.2 million.[10]

Other Union cavalry carbines include the Burnside carbine, invented by General Ambrose Burnside; the Smith carbine, whose barrel hinged down like a shotgun; the Starr carbine; and the Gallager carbine. The US government purchased a total of roughly 133,000 carbines of these four types alone.[11]

The Confederates lacked the machinery and facilities to manufacture breech-loading carbines in large numbers. The Confederate government hired small-scale gunmakers to copy foreign muzzle-loading carbines, such as the English Enfield Pattern. A muzzle-loaded weapon is one that is loaded at the front end of the gun. But as the war raged on, Union troops often seized Southern gun manufacturing factories. Scrambling to get their hands on whatever they could, Confederate agents were frequently sent to Europe to buy weapons and ammunition.

In 1862, the S. C. Robinson Arms Factory in Richmond, Virginia, began manufacturing a copy of the Sharps carbine known as the Richmond Sharps. The gun was not as well made as its Union counterpart, and it was never highly successful. In 1863, the Confederate government assumed control of the factory and continued production of the Richmond Sharps. Approximately 5,200 guns were made.[12]

An 1863 illustration shows Union forces firing Sharps carbines.

The South produced other breech-loading carbines, such as the Perry carbine, the Tarpley carbine, and the Maynard carbine. Each was essentially a variation on the Sharps design. The weapons were produced and issued in small quantities, so Confederate troopers often found themselves at a disadvantage on the battlefield. Instead, they had to rely on single-shot muzzle-loading carbines, such as the Springfield M1855 rifled musket. By the start of the war, however, the M1855—the standard-issue firearm of the US Army before the conflict—was already outdated and no longer in production. As in the case of cavalry sabers, most of the higher-quality carbines used by Confederate troopers were taken in battle.

PISTOLS

There were more kinds of handguns in the Civil War than any other type of weapon. They ranged from Revolutionary War–era flintlock pistols to single-shot pocket pistols to relatively modern revolvers. Neither the Union nor the Confederate armies designated an official pistol model. Many soldiers bought a handgun privately rather than using an inferior military-issued weapon. Some troops preferred carrying a handgun, while others found them too clumsy and undependable in battle.

The US government manufactured no handguns in its own factories. It bought what was needed from private companies. The government purchased 374,000 handguns during the war. Roughly 150,000 were manufactured in factories owned by Samuel Colt in Hartford, Connecticut, and London, England.[13] The most popular Colt revolvers were the Model 1851 Navy revolver, the 1861 Navy revolver, and the .44-caliber Army Model of 1860.

Several other notable arms manufacturers also supplied pistols to the Union. The Remington Arms Company provided the six-shot Army and smaller-size

Navy revolvers in different variations. The Starr Arms Company of New York sold the US government nearly 18,000 units of its .44-caliber Single-Action Army model.[14] The Savage Company, Rogers & Spence, and Eli Whitney Jr. were also major suppliers of handguns to the Union. The US government purchased handguns from abroad too. Roughly 40,000 handguns were bought from British gunmakers, such as the Adams Company. The French company Lefaucheaux sold the US Army more than 12,000 handguns.[15]

Similar to the Union soldiers, the Confederates preferred high-quality Colt revolvers. The Northern naval blockade of Southern ports, however, cut off the South from suppliers of quality weapons. The South was forced to manufacture crude, inferior copies of Colt models. The knockoffs were made in factories throughout the South, including

THE GUNS OF SAMUEL COLT

The weapons of Connecticut-born gun manufacturer Samuel Colt played important roles in the Civil War. In 1836, Colt received a patent for his invention of a revolving cylinder mechanism. The mechanism enabled a gun to be fired several times without reloading. Colt started a company to manufacture his new gun, called a revolver, and other guns he developed. During the Mexican-American War (1846–1848), he supplied the US government with Colt revolvers. During the 1850s, Colt did business with customers in both the North and the South. When war broke out in April 1861, he decided to supply only the Union army. This decision alone did not change the course of the war, but Colt's pistols would become the weapons of choice during the conflict. In 1873, ten years after his death, Colt's Patent Fire-Arms Manufacturing Company introduced the Colt .45-caliber Peacemaker model revolver. It became the most popular gun in the American West.

ELIPHALET REMINGTON II

1793–1861

Eliphalet Remington II was born on October 28, 1793, in Suffield, Connecticut. He became a blacksmith and worked at his father's forge in rural Herkimer County, New York. In 1816, the younger Remington built a rifle by hand, using parts he bought from a gunsmith and making the barrel himself. The rifle was highly accurate, and local demand for more of these rifles grew. The Remingtons began manufacturing the rifle, and the focus of the family's forge business shifted to firearms production. Eliphalet took over the business when his father died in 1828. He built a rifle factory in Ilion, New York, and expanded the operation to include pistols. Together with his son Philo, Remington introduced many improvements in weapons manufacturing. He died on August 12, 1861, shortly after the start of the Civil War. During the conflict, his company made thousands of arms for the Union, including the New Model Army and Navy revolvers. Today, the Remington Arms Company is one of America's oldest gunmakers.

Remington died just a few months into the Civil War, but the weapons his company built were widely used throughout the war.

those in Augusta, Georgia; Columbia, Texas; Columbus, Mississippi; and Memphis, Tennessee.

The South produced several original designs, but as usual, they were available only in limited quantities. The Spiller and Burr revolver was manufactured in Richmond and later in Georgia. Approximately 1,500 copies of the handgun were made. The LeMat revolver, invented by Dr. Alexandre LeMat of New Orleans, Louisiana, was designed to fire both bullets and shot. The Confederate government ordered 2,000 of these unique revolvers, but no more than 100 were made.[16] Despite the best efforts of the Union blockade, the South still managed to import approximately 28,000 British and French revolvers during the war.[17]

Superior weaponry, manpower, and availability of horses gave the Union cavalry a long-term edge over the Confederacy. Confederate cavalry officers, at least early in the war, were more effective leaders than their Union counterparts. They better utilized the cavalry units as a shock weapon and scouting force. By late 1863, the Union had vastly improved its mounted troops, probably by studying Confederate cavalry tactics. By mid-1864, the Union cavalry was as good as the Confederacy's.

Infantry made up the core of the Confederate and Union armies.

THE INFANTRY AND ITS WEAPONS

The infantry of an army consists of the troops who fight on foot. Infantry formed the largest part of both armies during the Civil War. At full strength, a Union or Confederate infantry regiment had 1,000 soldiers and officers. More frequently, however, the figure was closer to 750 men.[1] At any given time, the Union and Confederate infantry each numbered approximately 500,000 troops.[2]

Marching was part of each infantryman's daily life. Carrying 45 pounds (20 kg) of equipment and supplies, a regiment might travel three miles (4.8 km) per hour.[3] Heat, cold, snow, or rain slowed progress. Marching on uneven roads or rugged terrain could

THE GATLING GUN

Rapid-firing guns made their first appearance during the Civil War. The most famous of these was the Gatling gun, invented by North Carolina native Dr. Richard Gatling and patented on November 4, 1862. The gun had six barrels. When the operator cranked the handle, each barrel rotated into position and was fed from a sleeve that contained bullets. Once it began rotating, the gun could fire a steady spray of bullets across the battlefield.

Gatling wrote to President Lincoln about his invention. But the Gatling saw limited use during the war. Several Union officials believed Gatling was a Confederate spy, and the US Army even began investigating him. In addition, some Union officials did not see the tremendous potential of Gatling's innovative technology. Despite successful tests, the Union never put the gun into full service.

further reduce the distance a regiment could travel in a day.

RIFLES

The basic, most widely used infantry weapon was the rifled musket. Most were newly manufactured. Others were old-fashioned, smoothbore, muzzle-loading muskets that were converted to rifles by cutting spiral grooves into the inside of the barrel.

Early in the war, the standard Union rifle was the Model 1855 Percussion Rifle, manufactured at the Harpers Ferry arsenal between 1857 and 1861. Several thousand of these rifles were made, but many never found their way into the hands of Union soldiers. A Confederate raid on the armory in April 1861 destroyed many of these weapons.

Later that year, production of the Model 1861 US Percussion Rifle Musket began. These weapons became the standard Union infantry rifles. They were called Springfields because they were made in Springfield, Massachusetts, although many were also made at other factories. During the war, the US government manufactured more than 800,000 Springfield rifles and purchased an additional 670,000 from private manufacturers. The gun was durable, and it was deadly at battle ranges of 200 to 300 yards (185 to 275 m). In the hands of an expert marksman, the Springfield was capable of killing at 1,000 yards (900 m).[4] Improvements to the Model 1861 resulted in the Model 1863, of which the US government manufactured 270,000 pieces.[5]

In addition to supplying the Union with pistols as quickly as it could, the Colt Arms Company also manufactured revolving rifles. Two types of the Colt Model 1855 rifle were made: a five-shot and a six-shot. Colt sold nearly 5,000 revolving rifles to the Union army.[6] By 1863, the Union stopped using the weapon because of the number of accidents it caused. At times, two or more bullets in the revolver mechanism could go off at once, blowing apart the shooter's hand.

The fast-shooting Henry repeating rifle was a favorite among Union infantrymen. The gun was loaded with a tube that held 15 rounds, all of which could be fired in less than 11 seconds.[7] The Spencer repeating rifle, similar to the Spencer carbine Union cavalry used, was also widely used by the infantry, as was the Sharps breech-loading rifle.

Hundreds of thousands of rifles used by the Union infantry were imported from Europe. Nearly 430,000 British Enfield long rifle muskets were purchased

in addition to more than 8,000 short Enfield rifles.[8] The quality of these weapons varied greatly. Those manufactured at the government-run Royal Small Arms Factory in the London borough of Enfield were superior in workmanship. Those made by private armories were of poorer quality. The Confederates purchased many privately manufactured Enfields. Other foreign rifles imported by the US government included guns manufactured in Austria, Belgium, France, Prussia, and Italy.

The Confederate army started the war using some of the same rifles as their Northern enemy, mainly the Model 1855 and the Model 1842. Several small, private Southern gunmakers churned out copies of the British Enfield and the

A Confederate soldier poses with an Enfield rifle.

Springfield. Their output, however, was unable to keep up with the Confederate infantryman's needs on the battlefield.

The bulk of Confederate rifle production was conducted at three larger armories. The Fayetteville Armory of North Carolina produced several thousand copies of the Model 1861, at first using parts captured at Harpers Ferry. In time, the armory began manufacturing all the gun parts necessary to make the weapon. The second major manufacturer of rifles was the Palmetto Armory in South Carolina. The Richmond Armory in Virginia manufactured more carbines and rifles than any other Confederate armory. It produced three different models based on the US Model 1861.

SNIPING RIFLES

Snipers were formed into separate units or made part of other commands, either alone or in small groups. The most famous sniper unit in the war was Berdan's Sharpshooters, consisting of Union forces using the famous Sharps breech-loading rifle.

Snipers used the best rifles they could acquire, either by army issue or private purchase. In general, their weapon was a heavy-barreled rifle fitted with a telescopic sight. Often the sights were as long as the barrels themselves. For long-range sniping, many sharpshooters preferred a rifle much heavier than the Sharps, such as the J. F. Brown Sniper Rifle.

LOADING A RIFLE

A Civil War soldier had to complete a time-consuming process each time he needed to load his muzzle-loaded rifle. The process began with the cartridge. A cartridge is a type of packaging—paper or cloth—that contains a bullet and explosive powder. Millions of cartridges were used in the Civil War.

To load his rifle, the soldier picked up a cartridge and tore open the powder end with his teeth. He emptied the powder down the barrel and then pressed the projectile and the empty paper cartridge into the barrel with his thumb. The paper helped hold the projectile in place. He removed the ramrod, a long, thin metal rod, from under the rifle barrel and rammed the bullet until it pressed firmly on the powder. He returned the ramrod to its place and pulled back the hammer of his rifle.

BERDAN'S SHARPSHOOTERS

Hiram Berdan—inventor, engineer, and expert marksman—convinced Secretary of War Edward Stanton to allow him to organize units of specially picked marksmen. In late 1861, Berdan was named colonel of the First and Second US Sharpshooters regiments. The colonel recruited volunteers from eight different states, putting each man through a set of rigorous shooting tests. Berdan chose the Sharps rifle for his units. Their uniform consisted of a dark green coat and a green cap with a black ostrich feather, dark green or light blue pants, and leather leggings. The Berdan Sharpshooters were often used in skirmish duty. Berdan's men played an important role in the Battle of Gettysburg, delaying the advance of Confederate units from Alabama. They also fought at the battles of Chancellorsville, Antietam, Fredericksburg, and Second Bull Run, as well as in the siege of Petersburg, Virginia.

Then he removed a percussion cap with primer from the cap box on his belt and placed it on the rifle's lock mechanism. He was now ready to pull the rifle's trigger. When he pulled the trigger, a hammer slammed down on the cap, igniting the primer, which in turn ignited the powder in the barrel. The process was long and difficult, especially in rain or damp weather, and it could not be done lying down. Amid the smoke, noise, and confusion of battle, loading a muzzle-loading rifle was a risky process.

HAND GRENADES

Grenades saw extensive use in the Civil War. By 1863, grenades were being used in land warfare and on the seas to prevent enemy forces from boarding a ship. In 1861, William F. Ketchum invented perhaps the best-known grenade of the war. Ketchum's grenade was a cast-iron cylinder filled with gunpowder. It was fitted with a percussion cap on its front end that made the grenade explode on impact. Fins were attached at the rear of the grenade, and the grenade was thrown like a football. The Union army acquired approximately 93,000 grenades during the war.[9]

To make sure soldiers loaded and fired together at the same target, they were all taught to load, aim, and fire in the same way and only on command. The system armies used to teach soldiers these maneuvers, and to move them as a unit from one place to another in formation so they could fire together, was called drill. Armies drilled over and over between battles, following the rules of drill that were published in manuals of arms. Every soldier had to know his manual of arms to fight effectively.

The Twenty-Second New York State Militia drills at Harpers Ferry, Virginia, in 1862.

The more fortunate infantryman had a breech-loading rifle that used metallic cartridges with the bullet, powder, and primer all in one package. The cartridge was easily slipped into the breech. Even luckier soldiers had breech-loading repeaters such as the Spencer rifle, in which several cartridges were held in a tube that was loaded into the butt of the rifle.

Infantry was the backbone of both armies during the Civil War. Infantry endured the heaviest fighting and suffered the highest number of casualties. The infantryman's daily life was difficult and dangerous. Becoming ill from disease and infection was a constant risk. Camp life was boring, and the endless hours of drilling, marching, and standing at guard duty were often intolerable. But the fighting men on both sides survived as best they could, continually battling fear, panic, and uncertainty.

THE MINIÉ BALL

A DEADLY NEW BULLET

Before the invention of the Minié ball, the ammunition of muzzle-loading rifles had to be the same diameter as the barrel of the weapon. The user had to ram the bullet into the barrel by force so it would catch the spiral grooves of the rifling. A more efficient method of loading was needed.

In 1849, a French army officer named Claude-Étienne Minié invented a conical bullet with a hollow base that was smaller than the diameter of the barrel. The bullet slipped down the barrel without the need for ramming, even wrapped in its paper covering. When the iron bullet was fired, the explosion sent it hurtling down the barrel, expanding as it traveled. As it did, the bullet gripped the rifling on the inside of the barrel and spun tightly as it left the barrel and traveled toward its target. The result was increased accuracy and range. The Minié ball caused an estimated 90 percent of all Civil War casualties.[10]

A Minié ball with its paper cartridge

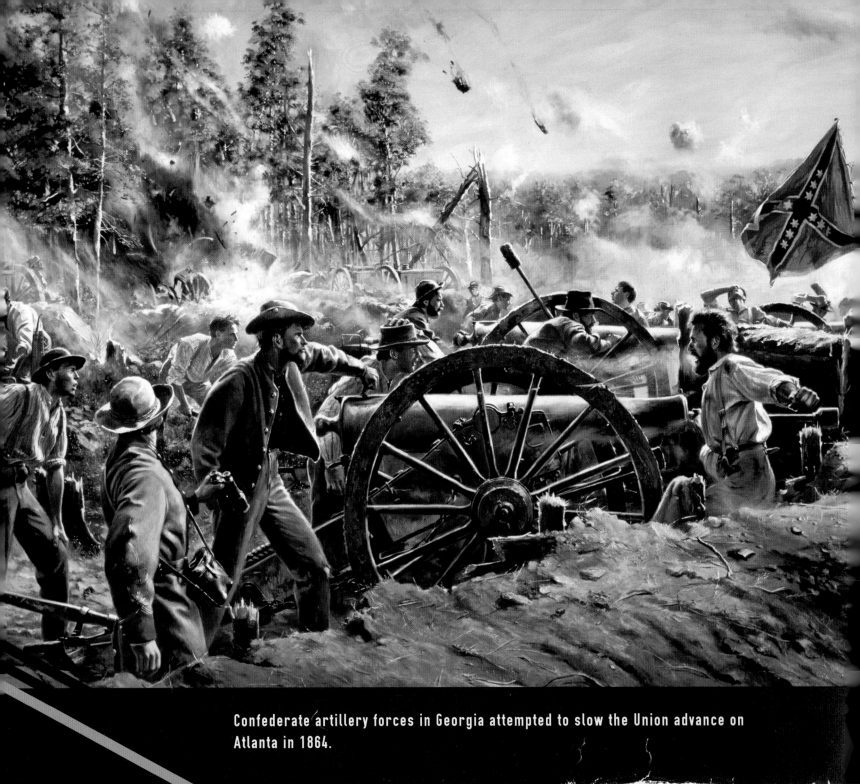

Confederate artillery forces in Georgia attempted to slow the Union advance on Atlanta in 1864.

ARTILLERY

Artillery pieces were the largest guns used during the Civil War, capable of firing projectiles over long distances with deadly effect. They include cannons, mortars, rockets, and other related weapons.

All cannons during the Civil War operated in essentially the same way they had since artillery was first used centuries earlier. The gun was a hollow tube made of iron, bronze, or brass that was open at the muzzle and closed at the breech. Most Civil War guns were smoothbore, but as the war progressed, artillery guns with rifling became more common. A bag of gunpowder was rammed into the muzzle and pushed toward the breech. Then the projectile was shoved in after it. Applying a flame or a lit fuse to a hole at the breech fired the gun.

CIVIL WAR ROCKETS

Two types of rockets saw limited action during the war. Confederate forces experimented with Congreve rockets obtained from England. The British used these weapons in the War of 1812 (1812–1815), mainly to set fire to buildings in Washington, DC. Gunpowder was packed into a metal case and attached to a long wooden stick. The rocket was fired from a carriage on the ground. Congreve rockets were highly inaccurate and were never widely used. Union forces used the Hale rocket, a metal tube that fired seven- and ten-inch- (18 and 25 cm) long rockets approximately one mile (1.6 km).[1] Although it was better than the Congreve rocket, the unreliable Hale also saw little use.

Artillery weapons produced an ear-splitting roar and a cloud of thick, blinding smoke that hung over the battlefield. They filled the air with the choking stench of burned gunpowder. As the projectile burst forth from the gun, it created a long trail of flame.

ARTILLERY AMMUNITION

Guns fired different types of ammunition. Solid shot had been the most commonly used for hundreds of years. Shot was essentially a solid, round ball of iron. It was most effective when it struck enemy artillery pieces or fortifications or landed among tight infantry formations. Shot was cheap and easy to manufacture, and it was simple to handle and load. Rifled guns sometimes used elongated versions of shot instead of spherical ones.

Explosive shells were used against buildings, defensive walls made of dirt, and troops under cover. They were fired from both smoothbore and rifled guns. A hollow shell, either round or cylindrical, was packed with gunpowder. In its base was a fuse made of a paper-wrapped strand of gunpowder. When the gun

Large stocks of artillery ammunition were stored at arsenals throughout the Union and Confederacy.

fired, the fuse was ignited. As the shell traveled, the fuse burned until its flame reached the gunpowder in the shell. When the gunpowder ignited, the shell blew apart into pieces.

Round case shot was used against large bodies of opposing troops at ranges from 500 to 1,500 yards (460 to 1,370 m). A thin, hollow ball was filled with

78 tiny lead musket balls and an exploding charge. When the case shot blew up above or amidst a line of troops, the balls flew in all directions. Most of the balls traveled into the air or into the ground, doing little damage. Those that struck soldiers, however, could be deadly.

The fourth main type of ammunition includes shot canister and grapeshot. Canister was a tin case packed with 27 iron balls held in sawdust. It was used at close range. When the canister exploded, the deadly balls sprayed in all directions. Grapeshot was made of larger balls up to two inches (5 cm) in diameter.[2] The balls were not packed in a case, but were instead held together in a cloth bag or by crude bands of metal.

CLASSES OF ARTILLERY

The three main categories of artillery were guns, howitzers, and mortars. Guns were relatively heavy, and they shot projectiles at long range on a flat trajectory. Guns usually shot standard solid cannonballs. Howitzers were lighter and had shorter barrels. They were designed to fire shells, often at higher angles than guns. Mortars were very short and heavy. They usually fired round shells on a very steep trajectory that brought the shells down vertically on their targets. This limited the mortar's range, but it made it effective at hitting enemies behind cover. Mortar shells had two holes for lifting tongs to allow soldiers to raise the shell and drop it into the upturned barrel of the mortar.

Mortars had short, extremely thick barrels compared to field guns.

Civil War artillery was also distinguished by the way in which it was used. Field artillery was relatively light and easy to move with an army as it traveled. Teams of horses pulled artillery pieces mounted on wheels. In battle, these guns could be quickly maneuvered into position. Mountain artillery was light enough to move up and down steep slopes and mountain ridges. Some mountain pieces could even be carried by soldiers or on the backs of mules.

Heavy artillery included the larger guns, which were often positioned around major cities, ports, forts, and other strategic locations. They included siege guns and siege mortars. In addition to firing shells, siege guns were often used to fire red-hot shot—heated before being loaded into the gun—against buildings or ships to set them on fire. Siege mortars were a type of short-barreled, smoothbore gun that fired shells at high angles.

Heavy artillery was often mounted on massive wooden or metal carriages. Forts had these guns on revolving platforms, which allowed them to be fired at different angles. Heavy guns were also used on ships to attack enemy vessels and bombard coastal towns. Naval guns fired shot, shells, and grapeshot. Some artillery was so heavy it could be moved only by rail or by sea.

THE ORGANIZATION OF GUNS

Both armies organized artillery into batteries. Batteries made up of either six guns or four guns were the most common. Batteries were further broken into sections. A section was composed of two guns. Therefore a six-gun battery had three sections, while a four-gun battery had two sections. At the start of the war, a six-piece battery included two howitzers and four guns of other types. Batteries were differentiated by the sizes of the guns they carried. A 12-pounder battery, for example, featured four 12-pounder guns and two 24-pounder howitzers. A 6-pounder battery had four 6-pounder guns and two 12-pounder howitzers.

A captain commanded the battery. A lieutenant was in charge of each section. Field guns were moved into action behind a limber pulled by a team of horses.

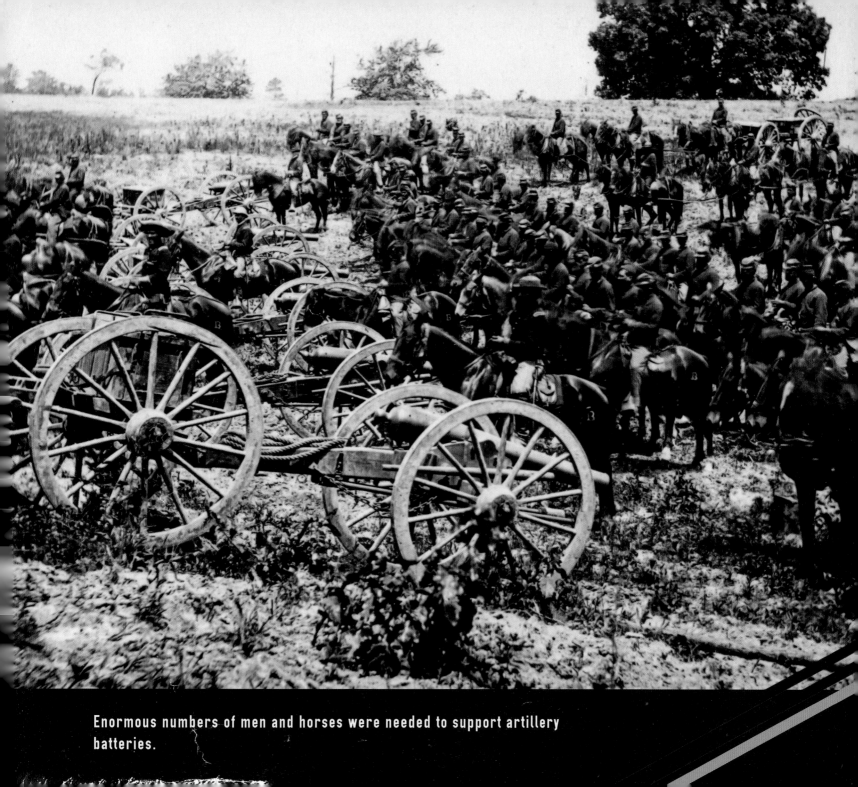

Enormous numbers of men and horses were needed to support artillery batteries.

The limber was a two-wheeled cart onto which the gun was secured. In the Union army, the horse team included six horses; four horses were used in the Confederate army. The limber also carried a chest of ammunition.

Each piece went into action with a caisson, which was attached to another limber towed by horses. The caisson carried two ammunition chests, a spare wheel, and other equipment. Each battery also carried a horse-pulled battery wagon. The wagon was outfitted with the equipment necessary to keep the battery on the move. It was stocked with repair tools, axes, shovels, picks, horse harnesses, and spare parts for wheels. It also had carpenters' tools, such as saws and chisels.

FIELD GUNS

The Model 1841 6-pounder smoothbore field gun was the workhorse of Union and Confederate artillery batteries. Hundreds saw action during the war, particularly during the first year of fighting, mainly with the Confederacy. The barrel of the Model 1841 was made of bronze and could fire solid shot approximately 1,500 yards (1,370 m).[3] The small projectile proved rather ineffective, however, and the field gun was later replaced by more powerful weapons. A 12-pounder howitzer version of the Model 1841, firing either shot or shells, proved more deadly, especially at close range.

The Model 1841 was largely replaced by the Model 1857 Napoleon 12-pounder gun-howitzer. Both armies had this weapon in considerable numbers, making it the most common field gun of the Civil War. As a gun-howitzer, it combined the long range of the Model 1841 with the more steeply angled shot of a howitzer. Made from bronze, or occasionally brass and iron in the South, the smoothbore Model 1857 fired every type of projectile available during the war: shot, shell, canister, and grapeshot. Its effective range was a staggering 1,600 yards (1,500 m)—the length of 16 football fields.[4]

ARTILLERY AT THE BATTLE OF GETTYSBURG

The Battle of Gettysburg, fought from July 1 to July 3, 1863, in Gettysburg, Pennsylvania, featured one of the largest artillery attacks in history up to that time. In the afternoon of July 3, Confederate guns began pounding Union positions in preparation for a full-on frontal assault. Among the weapons Confederate gunners used were the 12-pounder Model 1857, the 10-pounder Parrott Rifle, and the Model 1841 12-pounder howitzer. When the barrage finally stopped, Confederate soldiers began advancing on foot toward Union positions in an ill-fated assault later known as Pickett's Charge. Union troops beat back the attack, ending the battle. The next day, the Confederates withdrew and returned southward.

Many types of rifled field guns were in service during the war. Robert Parrott, an inventor and former US Army soldier, developed several models starting in 1860. Parrott manufactured his guns for the US government, while Southern foundries produced their own versions. Parrot's Model 1861 10-pounder rifle saw action early in the war on both sides. The gun was lighter than the Model 1857 Napoleon and had nearly double its range.

ROBERT PARROTT

1804–1877

Robert Parker Parrott was born in Lee, New Hampshire, on October 5, 1804. Parrot graduated from the US Military Academy at West Point in 1824. He was commissioned as a lieutenant in an artillery regiment and sent to the southeastern United States. There he served as a staff officer in fighting against Native Americans in early 1836. Later that year, he moved to Washington, DC, and served as inspector of the West Point Foundry. He resigned from the army with the rank of captain and accepted the civilian position of superintendent of the foundry in October 1836. There, just before the war, he began working on a process to build stronger cannons. At the time, bronze was too soft a metal, and cast iron was too brittle. Artillery pieces would occasionally explode, injuring their operators. Parrott solved the problem by wrapping a reinforcing band of wrought iron around the breech of a cast-iron barrel. Parrott's guns were inexpensive and easy to make and thus became popular during the war. In 1867, Parrott left his position at the foundry and turned over its operation to others. He continued experimenting with shells and fuses until his death in late December 1877.

Parrott's weapons saw widespread use both on land and at sea.

The Model 1861 3-inch Ordnance Rifle, developed by John Griffen and manufactured by the Phoenix Iron Company in Pennsylvania, was another popular and highly effective artillery piece. "The Yankees' three-inch [7.6 cm] rifle was a dead shot at any distance under a mile [1.6 km]," said a Confederate soldier. "They could hit the end of a flour barrel more often than miss, unless the gunner got rattled."[5] Made of iron, the 3-inch Ordnance Rifle was lighter than the Parrott, yet as lethal at the same range. The rifle was one of the most reliable and accurate artillery pieces of its time and served in the US Army until the late 1880s. Confederate copies of the gun were vastly inferior due to the lower-quality iron used in Southern foundries.

To compensate for its shortage of high-quality artillery pieces, the Confederacy looked to Europe, just as it had done for infantry and cavalry weapons. The United Kingdom was once again the South's largest supplier. British guns included Armstrong breech-loading and muzzle-loading rifles and 6- and 12-pounder Whitworth rifles.

HEAVY ARTILLERY

Prior to the Civil War, two types of the Seacoast Gun were used in forts that protected the nation's ports. Both the 32- and 42-pounder versions of these rifled guns were made of iron and had a range of nearly one mile (1.6 km).[6]

A large Columbiad nicknamed the Lincoln Gun was stationed at Fort Monroe, a Virginia outpost held by the Union throughout the war.

By the 1840s, these weapons were being replaced by Columbiads, extremely large guns capable of firing projectiles weighing up to 255 pounds (115 kg).[7]

Large Parrott rifles included siege guns, such as the 100-pounder, 200-pounder, and 300-pounder, the latter weighing a whopping 26,500 pounds (12,000 kg).[8] Both the Union army and Union navy used the large Parrott rifles.

The army used them to destroy enemy masonry forts, and the navy used them to harass ironclad ships from great distances.

Technological breakthroughs in casting iron gun barrels led to the development of even larger, more powerful heavy artillery. Inventor Thomas Rodman created a new version of the Columbiad, the Rodman Gun. The largest Rodman weighed 117,000 pounds (53,000 kg) and fired a 1,080-pound (490 kg) projectile nearly 3.5 miles (5.6 km).[9]

Artillery played a crucial role in the Civil War. A single blast from a gun could cause large numbers of casualties as well as strike widespread fear and panic into enemy armies. Artillery was capable of reducing well-built fortifications and large, modern cities to piles of rubble and debris. Such firepower made the Civil War the first truly modern war.

UNEXPLODED CIVIL WAR SHELLS

Unexploded shells from the Civil War have recently been discovered in several places on the East Coast. Private individuals and construction crews have found them buried in the ground or in areas with shrubs or brush. In 2015, a cannonball was found in the chimney of a house in Georgetown, Maryland. The unexploded shells can still be quite dangerous. In 2008, a Civil War artifact collector in Virginia was cleaning a Civil War naval cannonball in his driveway when it exploded. The blast instantly killed the man and sent pieces of the bomb flying a quarter mile (0.4 km) away. Civil War–era shells have also been found at former Union forts in Washington State.

Union vessels, *right*, attack Confederate forces at the Battle of Mobile Bay in 1864.

THE NAVAL WAR

Naval warfare during the Civil War did not produce the terrible large-scale battles with high casualties that were seen on land. Yet naval battles had a significant effect on the course of the war. The Union blockade of Southern ports, which began on April 19, 1861, restricted the Confederacy's ability to import all types of goods—including weapons—from Europe. In addition, the Union dedicated itself to seizing control of major waterways, especially the Mississippi River. Control of the Mississippi would cut the Confederacy in half, splitting the southeastern states from the western states. Union command of vital waterways also curbed the South's ability to transport goods by river.

WARSHIPS OF THE US AND CONFEDERATE NAVIES

In the decades before the Civil War, the standard warship was made of wood, fitted with sails and masts, and powered by wind. By the time the war began, a new technology, the steam engine, was beginning to transform naval combat. By 1861, many US warships were steam powered.

Around this time, the warship was undergoing a radical change in Europe. In 1858, the French began constructing the world's first ironclad warship. The ship had iron armor to protect against cannon fire. The next year, the British bettered the feat, building not only an ironclad ship but also one made entirely of iron. Union and Confederate leaders took notice and began considering the notion of an iron navy.

Immediately after the Confederate attack on Fort Sumter on April 12, 1861, the US government began a vigorous program of building new warships. The government also hired private shipbuilders

CONFEDERATE COMMERCE RAIDERS

Part of the Confederate strategy to beat the Union blockade was to use privately owned ships and its own navy to attack Union commercial ships at sea. Southern leaders authorized privateers to raid Union shipping. The privateers kept the cargo they seized as payment and divided the profits with the crew. In addition, the South arranged to have naval raiders built in the United Kingdom. The Confederate government paid the crews of these ships, so the sailors burned whatever cargo they seized. Some cruisers were extremely successful. The *Alabama* destroyed 58 vessels during its two-year career. In 1864, the USS *Kearsarge* sank the *Alabama* off the coast of France in a heated one-hour battle.[1]

to produce boats. Meanwhile, the Confederate navy had to be built from scratch. Many of the ships were bought from private owners in Southern ports, and when possible, others were secured from abroad. The South faced severe manufacturing limitations in its shipyards and foundries. Confederate naval authorities, however, were committed to the new and revolutionary technology of ironclad warfare.

IRONCLADS

On March 8, 1862, a strange-looking vessel steamed into Hampton Roads, Virginia, on a mission of destruction. The ship was a Confederate ironclad, the CSS *Virginia*. Previously the Union ship USS *Merrimac*, it had been captured and equipped with iron plating and other modifications. Armed with muzzle-loaded rifles and smoothbore guns, the *Virginia* opened fire on the Union ships blockading the harbor. In five hours, the ironclad sank two wooden warships and damaged another. *Virginia* returned the next day to finish the job, but it was met by the Union ironclad USS *Monitor*. For four hours, the two ships fired at each other at point-blank range. The shots dented the ships' iron hulls, but neither could sink the other. Although the duel ended in a stalemate, the historic first battle between ironclad ships had ushered in a new era of naval warfare.

The Confederacy built the *Virginia* by armoring an existing wooden ship. They continued to make ironclads this way, but they also built a number of

The *Monitor*, *right*, and the *Virginia* square off at the Battle of Hampton Roads.

ironclads from scratch. The CSS *Albemarle* saw its first action in April 1864, ramming and sinking a Union steamship on the Roanoke River in Virginia. Convinced the future of naval warfare was the ironclad, the Union built a fleet of 50 *Monitor*-like ships.[2] The majority of the Union navy still consisted of wooden

IRONCLAD GUNBOATS

Control of the waterways in the west was important to both the Union and the Confederacy. The large and small rivers were critical transportation and shipping routes. In mid-1861, the South built a series of forts in the west to control the rivers. The same year, the Union began building seven new ironclad gunboats to attack the Confederate forts and seize control of the waterways. The ships were steam powered and had paddlewheels. They were heavily armored, with 2.5 inches (6.3 cm) of iron protecting the 24-inch- (60 cm) thick oak sides of the boats. Each boat had 13 heavy cannons.[3]

The Confederates established the River Defense Fleet in 1861. Fourteen commercial riverboats were fitted with heavy, sharpened timbers to their fronts and used to ram enemy ships. In 1861, the South began constructing ironclad gunboats, but the ships were badly damaged in naval battles in 1862 at New Orleans, Louisiana, and Memphis, Tennessee. By 1863, not a single Confederate ironclad remained on the western rivers.

ships that traveled under sailing power, but the ironclads pointed the way toward the future of naval combat.

NAVAL GUNS

The standard naval guns on US warships in the 1850s were the 9-inch and 11-inch Dahlgren guns, designed by John Augustus Dahlgren. These guns fired both shells and shot as the situation demanded. The ironclad battle at Hampton Roads convinced US naval authorities the 11-inch gun was not sufficient against armor. In response, Dahlgren designed a 15-inch gun, which was mounted in the turret of the US ironclads then being built. The gun weighed 42,000 pounds

(19,000 kg) and could fire a 440-pound (200 kg) solid shot or a 330-pound (150 kg) explosive shell using 13 pounds (5.9 kg) of gunpowder.[4]

Gun designer Parrott developed special rifled gun designs for the Union navy, ranging from 150-pounders to 200-pounders. These guns, however, proved extremely unreliable. Many burst during the heat of battle. Some even burst while sitting on wooden supports in a gun yard without ever being fired. Dozens of Union sailors were injured or killed in the frequent accidents. The bursting was likely caused by poor workmanship in the foundry.

The Confederates used many Brooke rifles, muzzle-loading guns designed by Confederate naval officer John Brooke. The guns were manufactured in several sizes, including 7-inch and 8-inch (18 and 20 cm). Brooke rifles fired both armor-piercing and explosive shells. Armor-piercing shells were designed to penetrate the iron plates mounted on ironclads. They did not contain explosives but were intended to punch holes in an enemy vessel and cause destruction in its insides. The most successful armor-piercing projectiles used during the Civil War were made of a very hard iron alloy. Several Confederate ironclads were armed with Brooke smoothbores. The Confederates also acquired Blakely rifles from England in a variety of sizes.

Naval guns were mounted on heavy wooden carriages with two or four wheels. When the cannon fired, the carriage recoiled violently within the ship, rolling backward quickly and dangerously. A sturdy rope, called a breeching rope, was

Naval guns were sturdily secured, allowing crews to control the large recoil forces the guns generated.

passed through the rear end of a muzzle-loading gun and attached to bolts inside the ship. This helped control the powerful recoil of the gun on its carriage.

Naval ammunition was similar to army ammunition used on land. Solid shot was used more often, since its purpose was to shatter or penetrate enemy ship armor. Two methods of smashing through armor were used. Racking involved hitting the enemy vessel with large, heavy shot at low velocity. With repeated blows, the armor plating would fall off and weaken the structure of the entire ship. Punching involved smaller shot flying at high velocity to penetrate the armor and enter the ship, where it could damage the guns and harm the crewmen.

Solid shot was also used to pound and shatter the walls of coastal forts. Explosive shells were used against unarmored warships, riverboats, and other wooden vessels. Grapeshot and canister were used in close-range encounters against enemy ships, small boats, and groups of soldiers.

MINES AND TORPEDOES

By the start of the war, inventors had developed fuses that could set off underwater mines. At the time of the Civil War, underwater mines were called torpedoes; in modern militaries, the term *torpedo* describes underwater missiles that propel themselves through the water. The Confederates used torpedoes to destroy or damage ships and to strike fear into enemy sailors. Simple torpedoes were placed in waters where enemy ships would be on patrol or where an attack might take place.

The device might be a wooden, tin, or copper canister, or even a beer keg, filled with gunpowder. They were often simply left floating on the surface of the water or tethered with ropes and weights to float just below the surface.

Confederate torpedoes sank 27 Union vessels. Among the victims were four ironclad monitors and three ironclad gunboats.[5] *Ironclad monitor* is the general term for a low iron vessel with one or more gun turrets on its deck.

The Confederates also developed a new type of weapon based on mine warfare: the spar torpedo. This was an explosive charge attached to the end of a spar, a long, sturdy pole used for a mast on a ship. It was carried out on the water in small, fast, steam-powered vessels called Davids. Under cover of darkness, the vessel would approach an enemy ship and ram the explosive against it. Davids operated in the harbor off Charleston, South Carolina, causing great uneasiness among the Union blockading fleet.

While hundreds of thousands fought on land, the Union and Confederate navies were locked in a life-and-death struggle on the water. The war at sea was marked by technological breakthroughs, bravery, and bold strategy. As history reveals, the military that controlled the nation's waterways held the upper hand in the overall war.

THE COAL TORPEDO

One of the Confederates' most innovative weapons was the coal torpedo. This torpedo was a hollow chunk of iron made to look like a lump of coal. It was filled with gunpowder and sealed with wax. Then it was coated with tar and covered with soot. Production of the weapon began in January 1864 at a foundry in Richmond, Virginia. Confederate spies planted the bombs in Union coal supplies. When a coal torpedo was fed into the furnaces of Union steam ships, the gunpowder ignited and exploded the boilers. It is not known how many of these bombs damaged Union ships.

RECOVERING A SUBMARINE

The *H. L. Hunley* was a Confederate submarine launched in July 1863. During its test trials, the vessel sank twice, drowning crewmen in each instance. The ship's inventor, Horace L. Hunley, was killed in the second sinking. Each time, the ship was raised and returned to service. On the night of February 17, 1864, the *Hunley* sank the warship USS *Housatonic* with a spar torpedo. It was the first time in history a submarine sank an enemy warship. After the attack, however, the *Hunley* failed to return to its dock. The *Hunley* was not seen again until 132 years later. In 1995, a diving crew discovered the *Hunley*'s wreck in 27 feet (8.2 m) of water off Charleston Harbor. It was buried under several feet of silt approximately 100 yards (91 m) from the wreck of the *Housatonic*.[6]

In August 2000, the *Hunley* was raised from its watery grave, greeted by cheering spectators onshore and in nearby boats. The vessel was placed in a specially designed tank of water. Thousands of pounds of mud were removed from the wreck. Archaeologists uncovered artifacts, personal belongings, and the remains of the crew. To this day, scientists and archaeologists have not solved the mystery of why the *Hunley* sank. The leading theory is that the *Hunley* was too close to the *Housatonic* when the torpedo exploded. The concussion and shock wave from the blast severely damaged the submarine and may have rendered the crew unconscious. In either case, the crew could not respond quickly enough to save the vessel from flooding and sinking.

The *Hunley* underwent cleaning and restoration work after its removal from Charleston Harbor.

Union troops storm Confederate fortifications during the Battle of Petersburg in 1865.

FORTS AND FORTIFICATIONS

Field fortifications played a critical role in the Civil War. A fortification is a defensive structure built to strengthen and protect a place against attack. Field fortifications, or works, made during the war were generally temporary structures constructed from earth and wood. They ranged from simple trenches to walls of dirt, log blockhouses, long fences made from split timber, bombproof shelters, and more. Military engineers frequently combined various types of fieldworks at one location to create a complex network of fortifications and gun batteries.

CONSTRUCTION

The US Army Corps of Engineers and the Corps of Topographical Engineers were responsible for developing Union fortifications. The Corps of Engineers built field fortifications, erected temporary bridges called pontoons, and operated ferries to carry troops. The Corps of Topographical Engineers surveyed land and produced maps. They also carried out reconnaissance missions to provide information about the location and condition of bridges, roads, railroads, and river crossings. In 1863, the Corps of Topographical Engineers merged into the Corps of Engineers.

The Union army had an ample supply of well-trained field engineers. They performed their work by hand, using simple tools such as picks, axes, shovels, and wheelbarrows. They were also trained as infantrymen and were skilled at using rifles and muskets. Officers in the engineer corps had substantial previous experience as field engineers.

As in other aspects of the war, the Confederacy lagged behind its enemy. In the early years of fighting, the Confederates lacked a formal corps of engineers. The Pioneer Corps, groups of infantrymen gathered and supervised by experienced engineers, performed these duties. When Pioneer Corps men were unavailable, civilian men were put to work, often against their will. In one instance, 500 men were rounded up to help build a bridge on the James River.[1]

Union military engineers construct a bridge in Virginia in 1864.

The unlucky civilians were marched to their job under armed guard. The Pioneer Corps failed to meet the needs of the Confederate army, and so in 1863, an official corps of engineers was established. Despite the frequent shortage of men and supplies, Confederate engineers and soldiers managed to provide the South with well-constructed fieldworks.

Although African-American slaves were not allowed to fight in the Confederate army until the very last days of the war, slave labor was used in Southern military operations. Slaves built the trenches and defensive fortifications of key Confederate Virginia cities such as Richmond, Petersburg, and Lynchburg. Slave owners also rented their slaves to the Confederate government to be used as nurses and cooks in army hospitals.

CHANGING TIMES

In pre–Civil War days, American forts were massive structures made of brick or stone. They were built to defend coastal cities and were located at the entrances of harbors and the mouths of large rivers. The forts often had five sides and were equipped with two or three floors of heavy guns. They were further defended by surrounding moats and expanses of flat terrain facing inland. Enemy troops attacking the fort would have to cross this terrain, leaving them exposed to the fire of the fort's guns.

Such forts were built before the development of rifled artillery. They proved unable to withstand the pounding of heavy, accurate, rifled guns. Military leaders on both sides decided low-lying earthen fortifications would provide better protection against rifled artillery. The reasoning was simple. Earthworks would smother the incoming projectiles. Exploding shells kicked up great mounds of dirt, but the earthworks could easily be repaired. In addition, earthworks offered a flat target that would partially deflect incoming fire, unlike a hard stone wall, which could blow apart upon a shell's impact.

LARGER FIELD FORTIFICATIONS

Blockhouses, artillery stations, and bombproofs were among the many larger types of field fortifications that sprang up on battlefields across the country. Blockhouses were small, enclosed wooden or stone fortifications. These were especially useful to small units of soldiers stationed in remote locations as protection against larger enemy forces. The blockhouses varied from one-level squares to two-story, multisided structures that could house artillery.

Artillery stations were used both to attack opposing forces and to defend fieldworks. Cannons were often positioned behind parapets, protective walls made of dirt, sandbags, and logs. Heavy cannons were mounted on iron or wooden carriages and could be fired over the parapet. They could also be fired from behind embrasures, small openings in the parapet. Embrasures offered

BOMBARDMENT OF FORT PULASKI

The Battle of Fort Pulaski proved the effectiveness of rifled guns and changed the way Civil War fortifications were later made. Fort Pulaski was built by the US Army before the war. Constructed of brick and stone, the fort was located on a tiny island at the mouth of the Savannah River in Georgia, blocking access to the city of Savannah. In January 1861, state troops from Georgia seized the fort. In early April 1862, Union forces erected a series of gun batteries on the shore of the island to recapture the fort. The batteries included 20 cannons, including James and Parrott rifles, Columbiads, and mortars. On April 10, Union gunners began bombarding the fort. Within hours, the fort's masonry began crumbling under the blistering gunfire. By the next day, the bombardment had opened two 30-foot (9 m) holes in the fort.[2] With no hope of victory, the Confederate officer in charge surrendered.

Union soldiers stand outside a captured Confederate bombproof in Virginia in 1863.

protection for the soldiers operating the guns, but they restricted the area the cannon could reach by gunfire. Lighter guns were mounted on simple wooden platforms and were fired over or through the parapet.

Well-built bombproofs and shelters were erected on fortifications exposed to enemy artillery. Under heavy attack, troops could find relative safety in these sturdy structures. Bombproofs were sunk below the level of the ground. They had roofs made of thick timbers. The roof and exposed sides of the structure were covered with tightly packed earth. Openings were often made in the earth to provide riflemen inside the shelter with holes through which to fire. Ammunition and gunpowder were stored in specially made bombproofs to shield them from enemy gunfire.

Another important type of fortification was the rifle trench. A rifle trench was dug with fingers, tin cups, bayonets, or shovels. The inside walls of the trench were often fortified with timber or earth-filled straw baskets to prevent the walls from collapsing. As the war went on, trench systems often became complex networks featuring zigzags and earthen bombproof shelters. Firing steps were dug into the forward side of the trench, allowing troops to step up and shoot over the parapet.

SMALLER FIELDWORKS AND OBSTACLES

Many types of fieldworks were built on the outer edges of a fortification. These were frequently designed to slow the advance of attacking enemy troops. One type was

WHAT HAPPENED TO THE CIVIL WAR FIELDWORKS?

When the war was over, farmers took down fieldworks, cleared the land, burned wooden obstacles as firewood, and plowed and planted the battlefields. Families rebuilt their homes and barns on the land. Today, parks and woodlands occupy many of the places where Union and Confederate soldiers fought and died. Over the years, the US government has made numerous efforts to preserve Civil War battlefields. The National Park Service manages more than 70 sites related to the war.[3] Visitors can walk the grounds of Fort Sumter, Gettysburg, Bull Run, Fort Pulaski, and dozens of other historic battlegrounds.

A battlefield sketch by correspondent Alfred Waud shows Union infantry firing from a fortified position.

the cheval-de-frise. Invented by the Dutch in the late 1500s, cheval-de-frise consisted of a horizontal timber with two rows of sharpened wooden spikes. Several cheval-de-frise were often bound together with hooks and chains to form a long line of obstacles.

Another type of obstacle was the abatis. It was made by cutting down trees, stripping them of their leaves, and sharpening the branches into points. They were arranged on the ground side by side with the sharpened branches facing outward toward the enemy. Like any obstacle, the purpose of the abatis was to slow attacking forces so defenders could fire upon them at close range.

A breastwork was any type of protective wall that could be easily erected and from which a soldier could fire his weapon. Logs, rocks, and earth were typically used to provide infantry with protection to breast height. Breastworks were often made for an infantryman to crouch behind.

The Civil War witnessed an enormous development in the use of field fortifications. As the conflict raged on and improved artillery weapons became more deadly, fieldworks grew into complex, sophisticated networks of defensive lines. Upgrades to fortifications were frequent. The larger works surrounding the capital cities of Washington, DC, and Richmond were rebuilt numerous times.

THE DEFENSES OF THE CAPITAL CITIES

The divided nation's two capital cities—the Union's Washington, DC, and the Confederacy's Richmond, Virginia—were each protected by a series of complex earthworks. By the end of the war, Washington had 68 forts, 93 gun batteries, 20 miles (32 km) of rifle trenches, and 32 miles (51 km) of military roads.[4] Soldiers, former slaves, and other workers built the defenses.

Richmond was surrounded by three separate rings of defensive works. The outer ring was approximately 5 miles (8 km) out on the north and east of the city. The middle line was located 2 to 3 miles (3.2 to 4.8 km) out and was composed of 25 forts and batteries. The inner line was located just outside the city and ran for 12 miles (19 km). It included 17 forts and works for 218 guns.[5]

Union forces attack a Confederate defensive position at Fort Wagner in South Carolina in 1863.

CHAPTER
★ 7 ★

BATTLE TACTICS

Much of the fighting waged during the Civil War was between opposing infantry at close range. Military historian Paddy Griffith splits the infantry fighting of the Civil War into two different types. The first was attacking the enemy who held a defensive position, perhaps behind protective fieldworks or guarded by artillery. Battles fought in this manner were won by overpowering the opposition with continual and superior firepower.

The second was fighting a battle as a series of attacks and counterattacks. The outcome would depend upon shock tactics rather than firepower and protection. Hiding and then springing up and attacking with bayonets was one such shock tactic. Not firing weapons until the enemy was at close range was another. These types of fights were not necessarily intended to kill large numbers

THE REBEL YELL

The rebel yell was a battle cry used by Confederate soldiers during the Civil War. Confederate troops used the yell as they charged Union positions to terrify and confuse the enemy. There were many different versions of the yell. Recordings of former Confederate soldiers made in the 1930s indicate the yells were a high-pitched, shrieking squeal or howl. Some historians believe the yell originated with Native American cries. It was also possibly based on the cries of hunting dogs.

of troops, but rather to disorganize and confuse the opponent, driving him from the battlefield.

Union and Confederate armies fought on mountains, in woods, and along rivers and streams. Most of the fighting, however, was done on open fields. Long lines of soldiers marching shoulder to shoulder advanced toward the enemy in frontal assaults. The goal was to reach the opposition as quickly as possible in large numbers and overwhelm them with intense firepower.

In many instances, troops advanced to within close range of the enemy, stopped, and began an extended firefight rather than pressing forward. Prolonged firefights could wear down the enemy and pave the way for a successful frontal assault. In an age without instant communication devices such as walkie-talkies or radio transmitters, officers had limited control of the situation as it unfolded. Troops often moved forward, halted, and opened fire on their own.

The most widely used infantry formation was a long line two men deep, with one striding behind the other. Another common formation was the massed column. These lines ranged in depth from eight to twenty men.[1] On rough terrain, however, both types of formation often became too closely bunched together. This could result in the formation becoming a confused and disorganized mess before even encountering the enemy.

In addition, long lines and massed columns were already becoming obsolete in the early years of fighting. The widespread use of rifles firing Minié balls enabled the enemy to fire many accurate long-range shots before the attacking army got close enough to deliver a knockout blow. This made the frontal assault more dangerous than ever. However, the rifle did not ensure total success in every battle. Frontal assaults continued to be used throughout the war because despite advancing technology, an army still had to reach the enemy in some way. Battlefield experience showed that despite high costs, frontal assaults had reasonable chances to succeed. The Battle of Missionary Ridge, fought in Tennessee in 1863, included a frontal assault by Union troops that succeeded in smashing through Confederate lines.

A less risky but more difficult tactic was to attack the enemy from his side, or flank. Attacking armies tried to get around the end of the enemy line so they could fire on the length rather than the face of the opposition. This created a serious problem for the defenders. The flanked army would be unable to

More than 1,000 soldiers died in a single day in the Battle of Missionary Ridge.

effectively fire on the attackers without hitting its own men. Both armies used this maneuver during the war.

One of the most memorable flanking maneuvers of the Civil War occurred at the Battle of Chancellorsville, fought from April 30 to May 6, 1863. Confederate general Robert E. Lee sent Stonewall Jackson and his army of 30,000 men on a 12-mile (19 km) flanking march around the right side of the Union army. The attack stunned the unsuspecting Union troops, which led to a victory for the

Confederacy—perhaps its greatest of the entire war.

ARTILLERY TACTICS

Artillery tactics called for several batteries to be set up in close proximity in order to combine their fire on the target. Battery commanders tried to establish their guns at a dominant spot, usually the highest ground, before the enemy established his.

When encountering a frontal assault, artillery was most effective when fired at medium to close range. The goal was to destroy and disrupt the enemy before he got close enough to shoot back with accuracy. The deadliest effect of artillery came at very close range, roughly 300 yards (275 m). Napoleons or similar weapons firing canister could not only kill or wound the enemy but also stun and shock him with the noise and violence of their fire. These tactics often drove off enemy assaults and prevented them from reaching the defenders' positions.

Several new tactics using artillery were developed during the Civil War. Confederate artillery major John Pelham devised the idea of so-called flying batteries to trick Union forces into thinking he had a larger artillery force than

CIVIL WAR SKIRMISHERS

Skirmishers were infantry or cavalry soldiers who were positioned in loose lines in front of or on the flanks of the larger army. Their job was to harass the enemy, inflict damage, and disrupt formations before the main battle began. By attracting the enemy's attention, skirmishers could even force the opposing infantry into attacking too soon. Skirmishers were also used to test the enemy's readiness, allowing commanders to determine if a full-out assault was practical.

Confederate defenders sometimes disguised logs as artillery, hoping to make it appear as though they had more firepower than they really did.

he actually did. Using a four-gun battery, Pelham had his crews fire and then quickly move to a new position to fire again.

CAVALRY TACTICS

In general, cavalry units played a limited role in the major battles of the Civil War. It has been estimated that during the first three years of the war, only 1,400 Union cavalrymen in the eastern front charged Confederate infantry. These cavalry units suffered 365 casualties, or slightly more than one-quarter of their strength—a high rate of loss.[2] Rather than making assaults, the main mission of Union and Confederate cavalry in the early years of the war was scouting, patrolling, and guarding railroads and supply lines. Cavalry units were also used to guard the flanks of the army and protect it from surprise. If an army was forced to retreat, the cavalry served to protect the rear of the retreating troops.

As the war went on, however, cavalry were increasingly used for raiding rather than fighting in combination with the infantry. This new tactic incorporated several important features of the cavalry. It took advantage of their speedy mobility on horseback, their ability to dismount and fight on foot at closer range, and the availability of breech-loading repeating carbines with greater firepower. By 1864, cavalry was being used to capture key spots and make rapid hit-and-run assaults.

GUERRILLA WARFARE

As soon as war erupted, bands of guerrilla fighters sprang up in the North and South. Guerrillas operated outside the regular army. They conducted ambushes and surprise raids on enemy soldiers, cut communication lines, and destroyed railroad cars and tracks. Bushwhackers were Southern civilians who took up arms against the Union army. Many terrorized neutral or pro-Union citizens. Bushwhackers were a particular source of trouble because Union troops had no way of telling them apart from peaceful Southern civilians. Southern partisan rangers also operated independently, but they wore Confederate uniforms and reported to Confederate officers. Pro-Union civilians throughout the country, including the South, took up arms against the bushwhackers and partisans. They were called Jayhawkers in the Midwest and Buffaloes in the East.

Advances in technology contributed to the Civil War becoming the bloodiest conflict in US history.

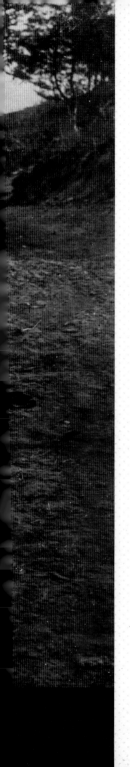

THE FIRST MODERN WAR

Historians have called the American Civil War the first modern war. New technology changed the very nature of warfare. The Civil War saw the first mighty battles between ironclad ships and introduced the submarine. Rifled muskets and artillery vastly increased the range and accuracy of an army's weapons. In his book *Trial by Fire: Science, Technology and the Civil War*, professor Charles Ross writes:

> *The Civil War took place right in the middle of [a] transformation from an ancient way of life to one not much different than that of today. As a result, the war became a laboratory for applying adolescent technologies to military situations.*[1]

Advances off the battlefield also changed the way the war was fought. The newly invented telegraph allowed for instant communications across thousands of miles. The railroad ushered in the age of mechanized warfare and rapid movement of troops, weapons, and supplies. Warfare would never be the same.

UNUSUAL CIVIL WAR WEAPONS

Not every new weapon designed during the Civil War made it onto the battlefield. Some were too strange—or dangerous—to see action. An inventor in the South designed a double-barrel cannon that shot two cannonballs connected by a chain at the same time. The barrels, however, did not fire at exactly the same time, causing the two shots to fly off wildly and land harmlessly far from the target. Two inventors from Ohio built the Winans steam gun, a massive weapon designed to sit on an armored train car and use steam to fire hundreds of shells a minute. The gun was a dismal failure and was never used in combat. Union forces seized the only copy of this odd invention in 1861.

WAR ON THE WIRE

By the late 1840s, the telegraph, developed by Samuel B. Morse and others, was spreading quickly across the country. It worked by using electric signals to transmit a series of dots and dashes over a wire. These signals could be decoded into messages. By the time the war began, thousands of miles of telegraph wires had been strung across the United States. The ability to communicate instantly over vast distances had far-reaching consequences. Military leaders used the telegraph to issue orders, coordinate troops, and even check on the activities of lower-level officers. For civilians, the telegraph permitted journalists near the front to file stories with

Telegraph workers often set up temporary field stations where they could send and receive urgent messages.

their newspapers back home, helping maintain public support for each side's fighting forces.

In February 1862, the US government took control of all the telegraph lines in the nation. The government formed US Military Telegraph (USMT), a civilian organization, to oversee these operations. The USMT employed roughly 1,100 workers, including foremen, wagon makers, messengers, and other laborers.[2] Some workers laid and repaired telegraph lines, often in hostile Southern territories. While performing their jobs, many workers were attacked by Confederate soldiers and Southern sympathizers. The government's aggressive construction program enabled the North to have a far more extensive and effective telegraph system than the South.

By the end of the war, the USMT had constructed thousands of miles of wire, including 76 miles (122 km) of underwater cables. USMT operators sent nearly 6.5 million messages during the war.[3] They made it possible for the United States to coordinate a strategy involving hundreds of thousands of men fighting in multiple armies across hundreds of miles of territory at the same time.

LINCOLN: THE FIRST WIRED PRESIDENT

Beginning in the late spring of 1862, President Lincoln used the telegraph to issue orders to his officers in the field. It was the first time in history that a commander in chief of an army had such rapid, direct communication with his military leaders. Lincoln spent many hours at the telegraph office located in the War Department building near the White House. The president used this revolutionary new technology to send nearly 1,000 telegrams during his presidency.[4]

In the South, news of secession from the Union spread quickly by wire. But the lack of wires and telegraph equipment prevented the Confederacy from significantly expanding its telegraph network. In late 1861, the Confederate government gave the president of the Confederacy, Jefferson Davis, control of all existing telegraph lines in the South.

Dr. William Morris of Tennessee was made manager of Confederate telegraph systems. The Confederates had no lines north of Richmond, but Morris kept information flowing throughout the South. In spring of 1865, as Union forces invaded Confederate territory, lines between Richmond and the rest of the South broke down.

WAR ON THE RAILS

The Civil War was the first war in which railroads played a crucial role, largely because the 1850s had seen a tremendous boom in railroad construction. By the start of the war, there were 31,500 miles (50,000 km) of track in the United States. Approximately 22,000 miles (35,000 km) had been laid in the North, with only 9,500 (15,000 km) in the South.[5]

Union and Confederate railroads carried enormous numbers of soldiers into battle. A city or town under enemy attack 300 miles (480 km) away could be relieved by an army in half a day by rail.[6] Such rapid movement of troops over great distances was one of the war's most important military developments.

Transporting goods, supplies, and equipment was an equally important function of the railroad. Throughout the war, railroads carried hundreds of thousands of tons of supplies to troops in the field. "The quicker you build the railroad, the quicker you'll get something to eat," Union general William Tecumseh Sherman told his men in 1863.[7] Sherman knew that without the railroad, his army would be in trouble.

During the entire war, not a single mile of railroad was manufactured in the Confederacy. When line was needed, it was taken from an existing track. The gradual weakening of its rail system contributed to the decline of the South.

Supplies were not reaching the fighting men. Shortages drained the Confederate soldiers' strength and their will to fight.

In addition to transporting heavy guns to the battlefield, commanders on both sides began mounting artillery on railroad cars for combat operations. The Confederates were the first to use artillery in this way. In June 1862, the Confederates mounted a 32-pounder rifled cannon on a railcar at the Battle of Savage Station in Virginia. The gun was protected from Union gunfire by a wooden shield covered with iron plates.

SHERMAN'S BOWTIES

Sherman's bowties were used to destroy railroads during the Civil War. Named after Union general William Tecumseh Sherman, bowties rendered Southern railways badly damaged and sometimes irreparable. To make a bowtie, Union soldiers ripped iron railroad rails from their wooden ties and placed them on a huge, raging bonfire. Once the rail was red hot in the middle, soldiers held it by both ends and twisted it around a tree, thereby creating a useless knot of iron. In a single day, troops could destroy as much as 10 or 15 miles (16 or 24 km) of train track.[8] Since the Confederacy had short supplies of iron and few foundries to manufacture new rails, Sherman's bowties were a significant blow to the Confederate war effort.

In time, ironclad railroad cars were in service. Light artillery pieces were fired through openings cut in the car while smaller gun holes allowed infantrymen to fire their rifles at the enemy. The rifle car was another innovation that made its appearance during the war. Rifle cars looked like ordinary cargo boxcars, but their iron plating was placed inside the cars. Troops within the car could fire from gun holes on all sides. Rifle cars were ideal for escorting supply trains and protecting railroad repairmen from enemy attack.

WAR IN THE AIR

Another major technological advancement made during the war was the balloon. Balloons had been a popular form of amusement at carnivals and fairs for several years before the war. In the summer of 1861, the US government authorized Thaddeus Lowe, a famous prewar balloonist, to organize a balloon corps. By early 1862, Union commanders were frequently using balloons to spy on

ENVIRONMENTAL IMPACT OF THE CIVIL WAR

All wars damage the environment. They destroy cities, homes, and farms, and they pollute rivers and lakes. They leave behind dangerous unexploded artillery shells. They spread disease. Hundreds of cities in the South were shattered beyond recognition. Charleston, South Carolina, and Vicksburg, Mississippi, suffered months of Union shelling. Atlanta, Georgia, was burned, and so was the South's capital, Richmond. Farms became battlefields strewn with trenches, bomb craters, fieldworks, and the bodies of dead soldiers. Entire forests were cut down to build camps and fortifications. Thousands of farm animals were killed during battle, while thousands of others died of disease and starvation.

Union forces inflate an observation balloon in June 1862.

Confederate troops in the field. Each manned balloon was controlled by a team of men with ropes on the ground. The balloons ascended upward, and people in the balloons observed from afar. Very few flights were made over long distances. The balloons could carry one to five passengers, depending on the size of the balloon.[9]

Telegraph wires were run up into the basket of the balloon. In a flash, a man in the balloon could telegraph back his observations. At first, the balloons were intended strictly for spying purposes. But soon the balloons became eyes in the sky for artillery batteries on the ground during a battle. Observers in the balloon were able to telegraph batteries below, telling them where their gunfire landed in relation to the target—right, left, over, or short. This allowed balloons to direct artillery fire onto enemy targets troops on the ground could not see.

The Confederates were eager to get balloons of their own into the air, but they did not have the means to make the necessary gas. Their first attempt was a balloon kept aloft with hot air. The balloonist managed to get airborne and drew maps of Union positions in Virginia. A second attempt was a balloon reportedly made from colorful silk dresses and inflated with gas obtained in Richmond. The balloon was tied to a train and driven to a good vantage point. There it reported on Union troop movements at the Seven Days' Battles in Virginia in late June 1862. The balloon was secured to a tugboat in preparation for another mission, but the boat ran aground, and the balloon was captured by a Union patrol.

THADDEUS LOWE

1832–1913

Thaddeus S. C. Lowe was born on August 20, 1832, in Jefferson Mills, New Hampshire. In his twenties, he studied balloon aviation, and he became a famous balloonist and builder of balloons. In June 1861, Lowe demonstrated to President Lincoln how his balloons could be used to spy on Confederate troops. The president approved Lowe's idea. On July 16, Lowe and his balloon were in service at the First Battle of Bull Run. Impressed with Lowe's performance, Lincoln authorized the establishment of the Union Army Balloon Corps with Lowe as its head. The Balloon Corps saw action at the major battles at Fredericksburg and Chancellorsville. But in 1863, Lowe resigned after funding for the corps was cut. He had also been accused of mishandling funds. Without its staunchest advocate, the Balloon Corps disbanded. After the war, Lowe became wealthy developing machines that made ice. He died in 1913 at the age of 80.

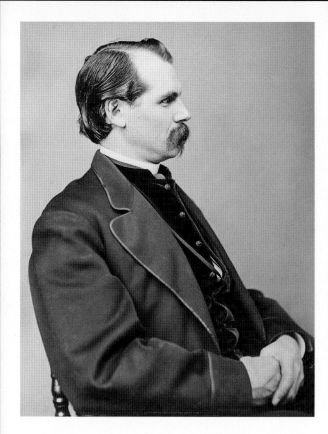

Before the Civil War, Lowe prepared for a transatlantic balloon flight, but the onset of the conflict halted these plans.

The Union balloon corps was disbanded in 1863 following Lowe's resignation. Confederate attempts at establishing a fleet of observation balloons ended even earlier. The war in the air was short-lived, but it had demonstrated the importance of such a technology in warfare.

In the decade from 1855 to 1865, weapon technology had advanced more rapidly than in the 80 years since the American Revolution. The list of breakthroughs is seemingly endless. It includes rifled guns, the Minié ball, repeating carbines, rockets, hand grenades, land and undersea mines, grenades, ironclads, submarines, and the Gatling machine gun. These developments made the Civil War one of history's bloodiest conflicts up to that time. Civil War weapons and their descendants would become critical elements of armies' arsenals for more than a century after the war's last shot was fired.

KEEPING THE PAST ALIVE

The field of Civil War photojournalism has provided generations of people an accurate look at that monumental conflict and all it touched—the soldiers, their families, the civilians, the battlefields, and the weapons of war. From the firing of the first shot at Fort Sumter to the surrender of the Confederate army at Appomattox Court House on April 9, 1865, photojournalists were on the scene to document the war's progress. The images they left behind have allowed historians to recreate the events of the war and to help people better understand why and how it was fought.

Thousands of photographers, including Mathew Brady, Tim O'Sullivan, brothers Daniel and David Bendann, and soldiers themselves, took more than one million photos during the war.[10] Thousands of images show troops on both sides: manning an artillery battery, training in open fields, playing cards, standing alongside the gun turret of an ironclad, cleaning rifles, performing mock saber fights in camp, and more. Photography was everywhere. And today it enables people to connect with those who fought the world's first modern war more than 150 years ago.

BRADY'S ALBUM GALLERY.
No. 552.

COMPLETELY SILENCED!
DEAD CONFEDERATE ARTILLERY MEN,
As they lay around their battery after the Battle of Antietam.

The Photographs of this series were taken directly from nature, at considerable cost. Warning is therefore given that legal proceedings will be at once instituted against any party infringing the copyright.

Photographers sometimes sensationalized their images with colorful titles or captions.

TIMELINE

1849
French army officer Claude-Étienne Minié designs the Minié ball, a projectile that results in greater firearm accuracy.

1860
The Spencer repeating carbine, designed by American Christopher Spencer, is patented.

1860
Robert Parker Parrott produces the first Parrott rifled cannon, an artillery gun that would be used in several sizes.

April 12, 1861
Confederate forces fire the first shots of the Civil war, bombarding Fort Sumter in South Carolina.

March 8–9, 1862
The ironclads USS *Monitor* and CSS *Virginia* fight the Battle of Hampton Roads.

April 11, 1862
Union forces seize Fort Pulaski, Georgia, effectively closing Savannah as a port for Confederate operations.

September 17, 1862
Union and Confederate forces fight at the Battle of Antietam in Maryland.

November 4, 1862
Richard J. Gatling receives a patent for the Gatling gun, the forerunner of the modern machine gun.

July 16, 1861

Union and Confederate forces wage the first major land battle of the war at Bull Run, Virginia.

1861

In the summer, the Union establishes a balloon corps.

1861

The US Army introduces the one-shot, muzzle-loading Springfield Model 1861.

February 1862

The US government takes control of the nation's telegraph lines.

April 30–May 6, 1863

The Confederates are victorious at the Battle of Chancellorsville.

July 1–3, 1863

The North and South fight the Battle of Gettysburg, the largest battle of the Civil War.

February 17, 1864

The CSS *H. L. Hunley* becomes the first combat submarine to sink a warship, the USS *Housatonic*.

April 9, 1865

General Robert E. Lee surrenders to Union general Ulysses S. Grant at Appomattox Court House, Virginia.

ESSENTIAL FACTS

KEY PLAYERS

- Mathew Brady was an early American photographer best known for photos of the Civil War.

- Thaddeus Lowe was a balloonist and leader of the Union army's military balloon corps.

- John Mosby was a Confederate cavalry officer and commander of Mosby's Raiders.

- Eliphalet Remington designed the Remington rifle and founded the Remington Arms Company.

- Christopher Spencer was the inventor of the Spencer repeating rifle.

- Robert Parrott was a US Army soldier and inventor of the Parrott rifle gun.

KEY WEAPONS

- Sharps M1859: This single-shot, breech-loading carbine could fire effectively at ranges up to 400 to 500 yards (366–457 m).

- Spencer repeating rifle: At the insistence of President Abraham Lincoln, the US government purchased roughly 94,000 breech-loading Spencer rifles.

- Model 1841 6-pounder field gun: This weapon was used heavily by both the Union and the Confederacy, especially early in the war. The gun was capable of firing solid shot approximately 1,500 yards (1,370 m).

- Ironclad warships: The introduction of armor-plated vessels changed the face of warfare forever.

IMPACT ON WAR

The Civil War was a period of great technological change. The new weapons that appeared on the battlefield, such as the repeating rifle, the Minié ball, ironclads, and mines and torpedoes, altered the way all future wars would be fought. New rifled artillery and firearms soon made the strategy of attacking the enemy in lines and massed columns obsolete. This style of combat gave way to trench warfare, which later became infamous in World War I (1914–1918). Steam-powered ships and submarines began replacing sailing ships. For the first time, railroads, the telegraph, and balloons played critical roles in war. This technological revolution heralded the transition to modern forms of warfare.

QUOTE

"The Civil War took place right in the middle of [a] transformation from an ancient way of life to one not much different than that of today. As a result, the war became a laboratory for applying adolescent technologies to military situations."

—*Charles Ross*, Trial by Fire: Science, Technology and the Civil War

GLOSSARY

ARTILLERY
A large gun manned by a crew of operators used to shoot long distances.

BATTERY
A coordinated group of large artillery pieces.

BLOCKADE
A military act in which one state uses its navy to block supplies from entering a warring nation.

CALIBER
The diameter of the inside of a gun barrel.

CARBINE
A firearm similar to a rifle but with a shorter barrel, making it easier to handle.

CASUALTY
A person who is injured, missing, or killed during a military campaign.

ILLITERACY
The inability to read or write.

PATENT
To obtain a legal document giving the inventor sole rights to manufacture or sell a physical item.

PROJECTILE

A bullet or other type of ammunition fired from a gun.

RECONNAISSANCE

An exploration of an area to gather information about the activity of military forces.

SHOT

A solid projectile fired from a cannon.

SKIRMISH

A minor battle between two groups of enemy troops.

SNIPER

An infantry rifleman whose task is to kill individual enemy soldiers at long range.

SURVEILLANCE

Close observation or watch kept over something or someone.

ADDITIONAL RESOURCES

SELECTED BIBLIOGRAPHY

Davis, William C. *The Illustrated Encyclopedia of the Civil War: The Soldiers, Generals, Weapons and Battles.* Guilford, CT: Lyons, 2001. Print.

Smith, Graham. *Civil War Weapons.* New York: Chartwell, 2011. Print.

FURTHER READINGS

Cooke, Tim. *Battles and Campaigns.* Tucson, AZ: Brown Bear, 2011. Print.

Crane, Stephen. *The Red Badge of Courage.* New York: Norton, 2007. Print.

Cummings, Judy Dodge. *Civil War.* Minneapolis, MN: Abdo, 2014. Print.

WEBSITES

To learn more about Essential Library of the Civil War, visit **booklinks.abdopublishing.com**. These links are routinely monitored and updated to provide the most current information available.

PLACES TO VISIT

Fort Sumter Visitor Education Center
340 Concord Street
Charleston, SC 29401
843-577-0242
http://www.nps.gov/fosu/learn/historyculture/lisqexhibit.htm
The Fort Sumter Visitor Education Center's exhibits include photos, maps, and artifacts telling the story of the fort where the Civil War began. Take a short ferry ride from the Visitor Center to the fort and explore the grounds, buildings, and weapons of this historic site.

National Civil War Museum
One Lincoln Circle at Reservoir Park
Harrisburg, PA 17103
717-260-1861
http://www.nationalcivilwarmuseum.org
The National Civil War Museum is the only museum in the United States that portrays the entire story of the American Civil War. Its collection features more than 21,000 artifacts, many of which portray the life of the average soldier from the North and South.

SOURCE NOTES

CHAPTER 1. TOOLS OF DESTRUCTION

1. "The Bloodiest One Day Battle in American History." *Antietam National Battlefield*. National Park Service, 16 Feb. 2016. Web. 17 Sept. 2016.

2. Benjamin T. Arrington. "Industry and Economy during the Civil War." *National Park Service*. National Park Service, 14 Feb. 2016. Web. 17 Feb. 2016.

3. "Civil War Casualties." *Civil War Trust*. Civil War Trust, 2014. Web. 17 Feb. 2016.

4. Guy Gugliotta. "New Estimate Raises Civil War Death Toll." *New York Times*. New York Times, 2 Apr. 2012. Web. 17 Feb. 2016.

5. "Who Fought?" *Civil War Trust*. Civil War Trust, 2014. Web. 17 Feb. 2016.

6. *Arms and Equipment of the Union*. Alexandria, VA: Time-Life, 1991. Print. 24.

7. "America's Wars." *Department of Veterans Affairs*. Department of Veterans Affairs, May 2015. Web. 24 Feb. 2016.

8. "Declaration of Independence." *National Archives*. National Archives, n.d. Web. 24 Feb. 2016.

CHAPTER 2. THE CAVALRY AND ITS WEAPONS

1. Angus Konstam. *The Pocket Book of Civil War Weapons*. Edison, NJ: Chartwell, 2004. Print. 116.

2. Ibid. 116.

3. Ian Hogg. *Weapons of the Civil War*. New York: Military Press, 1987. Print. 11.

4. Jack Coggins. *Arms and Equipment of the Civil War*. New York: Doubleday, 1962. Print. 58.

5. Angus Konstam. *The Pocket Book of Civil War Weapons*. Edison, NJ: Chartwell, 2004. Print. 74.

6. Ian Hogg. *Weapons of the Civil War*. New York: Military Press, 1987. Print. 12.

7. Jed Morrison. "Target Practice with Mr. Lincoln." *New York Times*. New York Times, 19 Aug. 2013. Web. 17 Feb. 2016.

8. Ian Hogg. *Weapons of the Civil War*. New York: Military Press, 1987. Print. 13.

9. John Walter. *Rifles of the World*. Iola, WI: Krause, 2006. Print. 438.

10. Ian Hogg. *Weapons of the Civil War*. New York: Military Press, 1987. Print. 13.

11. Ibid. 14–15.

12. Angus Konstam. *The Pocket Book of Civil War Weapons*. Edison, NJ: Chartwell, 2004. Print. 79.

13. Ibid. 89.

14. Ian Hogg. *Weapons of the Civil War*. New York: Military Press, 1987. Print. 25.

15. Angus Konstam. *The Pocket Book of Civil War Weapons*. Edison, NJ: Chartwell, 2004. Print. 90.

16. Ian Hogg. *Weapons of the Civil War*. New York: Military Press, 1987. Print. 29.

17. Angus Konstam. *The Pocket Book of Civil War Weapons*. Edison, NJ: Chartwell, 2004. Print. 103.

CHAPTER 3. THE INFANTRY AND ITS WEAPONS

1. Ian Hogg. *Weapons of the Civil War*. New York: Military Press, 1987. Print. 32.

2. Ibid.

3. Jack Coggins. *Arms and Equipment of the Civil War*. New York: Doubleday, 1962. Print. 23.

4. Ibid. 32.

5. Ian Hogg. *Weapons of the Civil War*. New York: Military Press, 1987. Print. 35.

6. Ibid. 36.

7. Jack Coggins. *Arms and Equipment of the Civil War*. New York: Doubleday, 1962. Print. 32.

8. Ian Hogg. *Weapons of the Civil War*. New York: Military Press, 1987. Print. 39.

9. Ibid. 55.

10. Angus Konstam. *The Pocket Book of Civil War Weapons*. Edison, NJ: Chartwell, 2004. Print. 26.

CHAPTER 4. ARTILLERY

1. Evan Andrews. "8 Unusual Civil War Weapons." *History Channel*. History Channel, 9 Apr. 2013. Web. 17 Feb. 2016.

2. William C. Davis. *The Illustrated Encyclopedia of the Civil War: The Soldiers, Generals, Weapons and Battles*. Guilford, CT: Lyons, 2001. Print. 277.

3. "Model 1841 6-Pounder." *Military Factory*. Military Factory, 1 July 2013. Web. 17 Feb. 2016.

4. William C. Davis. *The Illustrated Encyclopedia of the Civil War: The Soldiers, Generals, Weapons and Battles*. Guilford, CT: Lyons, 2001. Print. 281.

5. James C. Hazlett. *Artillery Weapons of the Civil War*. Newark, NJ: U of Delaware P, 1988. Print. 120.

6. "The Big Guns: Civil War Heavy Artillery." *Bugle*. Camp Curtin Historical Society, Spring 2014. Web. 17 Feb. 2016.

7. Graham Smith. *Civil War Weapons*. New York: Chartwell, 2011. Print. 237.

8. Jack Coggins. *Arms and Equipment of the Civil War*. New York: Doubleday, 1962. Print. 88.

9. Ibid. 88.

SOURCE NOTES
CONTINUED

CHAPTER 5. THE NAVAL WAR

1. John M. Browne. "The Duel Between the *Alabama* and the *Kearsarge*." *Civil War Trust*. Civil War Trust, 2014. Web. 17 Feb. 2016.

2. "Ironclad Warships." *American Civil War Story*. American Civil War Story, n.d. Web. 17 Feb. 2016.

3. "Ironclad Gunboats." *Fort Donelson National Battlefield*. National Park Service, 17 Feb. 2016. Web. 17 Feb. 2016.

4. Ian Hogg. *Weapons of the Civil War*. New York: Military Press, 1987. Print. 116.

5. Jack Coggins. *Arms and Equipment of the Civil War*. New York: Doubleday, 1962. Print. 146.

6. "The Loss of Confederate Ship *Hunley*." *Submarine Force Museum*. Submarine Force Museum, 2013. Web. 17 Feb. 2016.

CHAPTER 6. FORTS AND FORTIFICATIONS

1. Jack Coggins. *Arms and Equipment of the Civil War*. New York: Doubleday, 1962. Print. 99.

2. David H. McGee. "Fort Pulaski." *New Georgia Encyclopedia*. Georgia Humanities Council, 9 Sept. 2014. Web. 17 Feb. 2016.

3. "Civil War Parks." *National Park Service*. National Park Service, n.d. Web. 17 Feb. 2016.

4. "Civil War Defenses of Washington." *Civil War Traveler*. Civil War Traveler, n.d. Web. 17 Feb. 2016.

5. "Civil War Defenses of Richmond." *North American Forts*. North American Forts, 12 Oct. 2014. Web. 17 Feb. 2016.

CHAPTER 7. BATTLE TACTICS

1. "Tactics." *Civil War Home.* Civil War Home, 26 Mar. 2005. Web. 17 Feb. 2016.

2. Paddy Griffith. *Battle Tactics of the Civil War.* New Haven, CT: Yale UP, 1989. Print. 180.

CHAPTER 8. THE FIRST MODERN WAR

1. Charles Ross. *Trial by Fire: Science, Technology and the Civil War.* Shippensburg, PA: White Mane, 2000. Print. ix.

2. Ibid. 153.

3. Ibid. 162.

4. "In the Original Situation Room—Abraham Lincoln and the Telegraph." *Civil War Studies.* Smithsonian Associates, 2012. Web. 18 Feb. 2016.

5. "Railroads of the Confederacy." *Civil War Trust.* Civil War Trust, 2014. Web. 18 Feb. 2016.

6. Ian Drury and Tony Gibbons. *The Civil War Military Machine: Weapons and Tactics of the Union and Confederate Armed Forces.* New York: Smithmark, 1993. Print. 82.

7. *The American Heritage Picture History of the Civil War.* New York: American Heritage, 1960. Print. 411.

8. "Sherman's Bowties." *Civil War Home.* Civil War Home, 30 Jan. 2003. Web. 18 Feb. 2016.

9. "Civil War Ballooning." *Civil War Trust.* Civil War Trust, 2014. Web. 18 Feb. 2016.

10. Ted Widmer. "Cameristas." *New York Times.* New York Times, 2 May 2013. Web. 18 Feb. 2016.

INDEX

African Americans, 10, 69–70
Albemarle, CSS, 58
Antietam, Battle of, 5–6, 34
artillery, 41–53
  Columbiads, 52–53, 71
  guns, 44
  howitzers, 44, 46, 48–49
  mortars, 44, 46, 71
  rockets, 42
artillery ammunition, 42–44
  explosive shells, 42–43, 60, 62
  grapeshot, 6, 44, 46, 49, 62
  round case shot, 43–44
  shot, 42
  shot canister, 44

balloons, 12, 91–95
batteries, 5, 46–48, 67, 71, 75, 81–82, 93, 96
Berdan's Sharpshooters, 33, 34
breech loading, 20, 37
Brooke, John, 60

caissons, 48
carbines, 19–24
  Enfield Pattern, 22
  Richmond Sharps, 22–23
  Sharps M1859, 21–22
  Spencer repeating rifle, 20–21
  Springfield M1855, 24
  US Pistol Carbine Model 1855, 20
casualties, 6, 9, 13, 38, 82
cavalry, 15–27

Colt, Samuel, 20, 24–25
commerce raiders, 56

Dahlgren, John Augustus, 59
Declaration of Independence, 13
drill, 35–37

engineers, 34, 67–69
environmental impact, 91

Fayetteville Armory, 33
fieldworks, 73–75
  abatis, 74–75
  breastwork, 75
  cheval-de-frise, 73–74
foreign weapons, 18, 22, 25, 27, 31–32, 51, 60
Fort Pulaski, 71, 73
Fort Sumter, 56
fortifications, 71–73
  artillery stations, 71–72
  blockhouses, 71
  bombproofs, 72–73
  earthworks, 70
  rifle trenches, 73

Gatling gun, 30
Gettysburg, Battle of, 34, 49, 73
guerrilla warfare, 83
gunboats, 59, 63

H. L. Hunley, CSS, 64
hand grenades, 35
handguns, 24–27
Harpers Ferry, 11, 12, 30, 33

infantry, 29–39
ironclads, 12, 53, 56–60, 63, 85

lances, 18–19
Lee, Robert E., 12, 80
limbers, 46–48
Lincoln, Abraham, 20, 30, 88, 94
Lowe, Thaddeus, 93–95

manuals of arms, 35
Mexican-American War, 25
mines, 62–63
Minié ball, 38
Mississippi River, 55
Monitor, USS, 57–58
Morris, William, 89
Mosby, John, 16
muzzle loading, 22, 34–35, 38, 41

naval blockade, 25, 27, 55, 56, 63

Palmetto Armory, 33
Parrott, Robert, 49–51, 52, 60, 71
photography, 8, 96

railroads, 8, 68, 83, 86, 89–91
rebel yell, 78
Remington, Eliphalet, II, 26
Remington Arms Company, 24–25
Revolutionary War, 12, 13, 24
Richmond, Virginia, 22, 27, 63, 70,
 75, 89, 91, 93
Richmond Armory, 33
rifled weapons, 19
rifles, 30–37
    Colt Model 1855, 31
    Enfield, 31–32
    Henry repeating rifle, 31
    Model 1842, 32
    Model 1855 Percussion Rifle, 30
    Model 1861 Percussion Rifle
     (Springfield), 30–31
    Model 1863 Percussion Rifle, 31
Rodman, Thomas, 53

sabers, 17–19
    Model 1840, 17
    Model 1860, 17
    Pattern 1853, 18
Sherman, William Tecumseh, 90
smoothbore weapons, 19
sniper rifles, 33, 34
soldiers' backgrounds, 10
Spencer, Christopher M., 20
submarines, 64

tactics, 77–83
    artillery tactics, 81–82
    cavalry tactics, 82–83
    flanking, 79–81
    formations, 79
    infantry tactics, 77–81
    skirmishers, 81
telegraphs, 86–89
torpedoes. *See* mines

unexploded shells, 53, 91

Virginia, CSS, 57

War of 1812, 42
warships, 55–59
    armoring, 57–59
    weapons, 59–62
Washington, DC, 42, 50, 75
Wilder, John Thomas, 21

ABOUT THE AUTHOR

Nel Yomtov is an award-winning author of nonfiction books and graphic novels for young readers. His writing passions include history, military, geography, sports, nature, biographies, and careers. Yomtov has also written, edited, and colored hundreds of comic books for Marvel Comics. He has served as editorial director of a large children's nonfiction book publisher and as an executive editor of Hammond World Atlas book division. As a full-time consultant, Nel also helped develop and implement an educational program for Major League Baseball, distributed to schools throughout the United States. Nel lives in the New York City area with his wife, Nancy.